Collaborative MINISTRY

Collaborative MINISTRY

What it is, how it works and why

DAVID ROBERTSON

Published by
The Bible Reading Fellowship
First Floor, Elsfield Hall
15–17 Elsfield Way, Oxford OX2 8FG
Website: www.brf.org.uk

ISBN-10: 1 84101 493 1
ISBN-13: 978 1 84101 493 7
First published 2007
10 9 8 7 6 5 4 3 2 1 0

Acknowledgments
Unless otherwise stated, scripture quotations are taken from the Holy Bible, New International Version, copyright © 1973, 1978, 1984, 1995 by International Bible Society, and are used by permission of Hodder & Stoughton Limited. All rights reserved. 'NIV' is a registered trademark of International Bible Society. UK trademark number 1448790.

A catalogue record for this book is available from the British Library

Printed in Singapore by Craft Print International Ltd

CONTENTS

FOREWORD

Partnership is a buzz word, not only in political circles but also in the church. Ever since the publication over 40 years ago of *God's Frozen People*, the need for Collaborative Ministry has been acknowledged; the thaw is happening, but not quickly enough.

David Robertson takes us to the theological heart of the matter by reminding us that Collaborative Ministry, properly understood, is about grace. God is not a loner but a social God, who graciously invites his creatures to share in the life of the Trinity. Our participation in the divine life is the sole rationale for ministry of any kind. As the apostle Paul says, we are 'workers together with God'—and we might well add 'not *for God*'.

This book emerges out of the life of an ordinary parish where the Christian community, along with the author, has started to learn some of the lessons that are offered for our instruction. This is much more than a manual on ministry. It challenges us to re-examine what it means for our church life, and all that flows from that, to be genuinely Christ-centred. It is rigorous in its examination of the biblical material and thoroughly practical in its application.

Ministry is a communal activity, and the risen Christ invites us to learn from him within the fellowship of his church. It could be, therefore, that the best way to use this book is in group discussion. Collaborative Ministry, after all, is not about gimmicks, techniques or strategies but about relationships.

Fundamental to this challenge is the need for scripture to be allowed to speak with fresh clarity. I suspect that those who are prepared to do the hard work set at the end of each chapter will be those who benefit most from this exciting and sometimes quirky look at a well-worn theme.

+ Colin Coventry

INTRODUCTION

THE CURRENT VIEW

At the time of writing, Collaborative Ministry (CM) is fast becoming a 'buzz phrase' in the church. It appears in ordination services, and is commonly used by churches when they advertise for a new minister. It is referred to by those who speak and write about leadership, the church and outreach. It is usually, however, mentioned in passing and rarely defined. That's the problem with a buzz phrase: if it's widely used, everyone thinks they know what it means, nods wisely when it's used... and interprets it to mean just about anything! If this continues for any length of time, the buzz phrase turns into a bandwagon and, as a multitude of meanings leap on to it, the concept underlying the original phrase quietly collapses under the strain.

The current view is that CM is a good thing, and a solution to most of our problems. It is, allegedly, the answer to the declining numbers of clergy, ministers and church leaders, and will also solve the decline in church membership. Similarly, it is widely thought that large churches are doing fine—engaging in CM and getting on with being successful—while small churches need to get their act together and begin CM as soon as possible.

This book will not only consider CM but also define it and explore the theology and practice of this style of 'being church'. In the process, it will question the current view, consider the implications for both large and small churches, and study the Bible to provide a secure foundation.

A CURRENT ASSUMPTION

Added to the current view that CM is a good thing is the assumption that CM can be 'bolted on' to existing leadership structures. This may or may not be true: it all depends on the shape of the original structure and whether or not CM is compatible with it. If the two are incompatible, then simply adding CM may strain the existing leadership to the point of collapse. In practice, and in the local situation, this may mean that we can't bolt CM on to what we already have: the choice is then either to leave well alone or to demolish and rebuild. Similarly, our leadership structures may be located in a culture that is no longer relevant to most people—perhaps only to a small minority. If this is the case, even sound, solidly built leadership structures will be isolated from the culture around us.

This book is written in three parts:

- Part One compares the CM approach with existing church leadership structures. This can be thought of as a structural survey.
- Part Two looks at the biblical themes of authority (leadership), acceptance (membership) and covenant (the relationship between the two). These Bible studies define CM and form a foundation on which it can be built.
- Part Three examines the practicalities of rebuilding a leadership structure.

It is not necessary to read this book in order. It is possible to go straight to Part Three, begin with Part Two, or read each section in parallel. As a general rule, though, it would be wise to read it as presented, in order. That way, the survey is considered first, which will give some idea of how extensive the job might be. Then the foundations are defined and attended to—and they might need underpinning, totally replacing or laying somewhere else. Finally, and only when ready, do we build.

There are questions for discussion at the end of each chapter in Part One. Also, questions for group study (relating to Chapters 5 to 11) are provided at the end. These may be freely reproduced for group discussion (or wider circulation) in a church considering the move towards a collaborative approach.

IS COLLABORATIVE MINISTRY NEW?

In the 1990s, CM was called 'enabling'. In the previous decade it was called 'shared ministry', before that 'every-member ministry' and before that 'the priesthood of all believers'. Interestingly, what-ever it was called, it made little impact. This is probably because CM has always been regarded as a side issue or a bolt-on to the central task of leadership, the assumption being, 'But we're all doing this any-way... aren't we?' This book will examine not only CM but also what happens when it becomes central to a leadership structure.

In the church, most leadership models rely on delegation, and in recent years secular management techniques have shed some helpful light on these models. In the secular business world, 'partner-ships' are the closest models to CM, but the two are not identical. In the partnership model (for example, in a group of solicitors or general practitioners), each partner gets on with his or her own job and they only confer over points of difficulty. They meet to discuss policy and meetings are chaired by the senior partner, but on a day-to-day basis they trust each other to get on with the corporate task. In a church context, this kind of leadership structure could be termed Collaborative Leadership (CL) because ministers work in partnership and collaborate with each other. They do not, however, behave collaboratively with their members (any more than solicitors or doctors collaborate with their clients).

By contrast, CM is a structure that includes both ministers and members. This highlights the shortcomings of secular models: because existing church leadership structures have grown out of a particular theology, it will not suffice simply to import a management philosophy into the church. CM is not a management technique. It is not a new way to run the same old leadership structure but a practical development of a theology of leadership, which rests on a particular theology of church. Therefore, it is helpful to consider the existing theology of leadership that underpins current practice and compare it with the theology of CM. Only then shall we appreciate why a CM structure looks different from a traditional leadership structure.

Unless the 'why' of CM (the theology) is understood, we shall imagine that we can engage in it without making any changes to fundamental attitudes. At that point, we can end up embracing the theory while disregarding the practice.

WORKING WITH OTHERS

All human activity involving more than one person requires some kind of organization. Children quickly work out who is leading a game and who is following—and when there are different opinions about who is in charge (or arguments about the precise rules of the game) an interesting facet of human behaviour emerges. Without care, it's possible to spend so much time organizing the leadership structure that no time is left to play the game. Growing up, we learn that organized leadership is better than anarchy and that there is an appropriate ratio of leaders to followers in most situations. When the group is small, only one leader is needed; when the group is large (perhaps a nation), a vast number may be necessary.

Whatever their size, organizations of human beings tend to fall under one of three different leadership styles:

- **Autocracy** accepts that one person holds power and makes decisions.
- **Delegation** expects this one person to share their power and decision-making with others.

- **Collaboration** recognizes that each person has power and the ability to make decisions—and expects each one to contribute to the whole.

Any of these three styles of leadership can be thought of as collaborative: even in an autocracy, the majority have to allow the top man to lead. If they refuse to do as he says, he is the leader of no one. Autocracy and collaboration are opposite approaches, however, because the former requires the many to accept the personal authority of the leader, while the latter requires the leader to accept the personal authority of the many. Somewhere between these two opposites is delegation—although its roots are in autocracy, not collaboration, because delegation looks to a hierarchical leader whereas collaboration does not.

Three key aspects

In the church we may be familiar with a pattern of ministry that is autocratic, delegated or collaborative, but there are three key aspects that apply to every leadership structure.

1. **Authority:** Depending on the church tradition, the local church leader may be called a minister, priest, elder, vicar, apostle, prophet or some other descriptive title. Whatever the title, it means that this is the person who is in charge of the people described in '2' below, and the person who holds authority.
2. **Acceptance:** Again, depending on tradition, the gathering of people in a local church may be called a congregation, fellowship, membership or some other descriptive title—meaning that these are the people who accept the authority of the person described in '1' above.
3. **Covenant:** This is the relationship between the leader ('1') and the people ('2').

In terms of a theology of leadership, it matters whether the emphasis is placed on authority or acceptance. If a structure for leadership rests primarily on attitudes to the leaders, it will look very different from a structure that rests on ideas about the members. To use political systems as an example, a nation that emphasizes authority is at the fascist end of the spectrum while a nation that emphasizes acceptance is at the communist end.

In this book, these aspects of authority and acceptance are examined from a biblical perspective and it is suggested that CM describes an appropriate covenant for the church.

TEACH IT; DO IT

Why am I writing about CM? Because the theology of CM has shaped my thinking and practice. I was ordained in 1979 and, as a curate, I joined a staff of six. When I moved, it was to an ecumenical team ministry of five clergy. My next move was to another team ministry, this time with (at its peak) eleven clergy. When I arrived in Halifax in 1997, there were six on the staff. In each of these places, the clergy worked together and, by many definitions of ministry, were collaborative—but it was CL, Collaborative Leadership. For the past 20 years, however, I have been engaged in a form of CM that is concerned with the whole church, where ordained, lay, accredited leaders and 'ordinary' members work and lead together.

Even the least observant reader will have spotted that I am a vicar in the Church of England and may be asking, 'So is this book aimed at the Anglican Church?' No. This book is about biblical principles, and it doesn't matter which denomination our church is part of: the issues we face are the same. When I refer to church structures, they will be Anglican structures, but they can be considered as an example rather than as a pattern. Whichever denomination we belong to, there's hope. After all, if CM can be done within the Church of England, then it can be pursued anywhere!

Also, if my brief history suggests that I have always ministered in 'large' churches, this would be a false impression. Two have been large, one had a congregation of fewer than 20, and the rest have been middle sized. In each one, though, we lived through change. In Halifax I am now the only full-time paid member of staff, but I minister in a collaborative structure with leaders generated from within the congregation (at the time of writing, two Ordained Local Ministers, two Readers, six people who hold the Bishop's Pastoral Certificate, lay leaders and group leaders). Similarly, the churches have been in rural, suburban and urban priority areas (or inner-city communities), and CM is appropriate to each.

In the following chapters, for simplicity, the word 'minister' will be used to describe the 'priest', 'vicar', 'church leader' and so on; also, for brevity, all leaders will be designated as male. This isn't because one term is correct or that only men should lead—it just means that we don't have to struggle through a whole list of titles or gender acknowledgment on each occasion.

READ IT; DO IT

This book is not a blueprint; it's a contribution. It looks at some of the principles involved in being a collaborative church and offers ideas and tools to help with the process. It suggests a direction and points out some of the crossroad decisions, but this book will not make CM happen. If a church wishes to pursue CM, it must do the work itself.

✣

Chapter 1

IN THE SHADOW OF PYRAMIDS

When it comes to leadership structures, the pyramid is the most common form. It can be seen in the family, the tribe, and the nation.

It can look very simple:

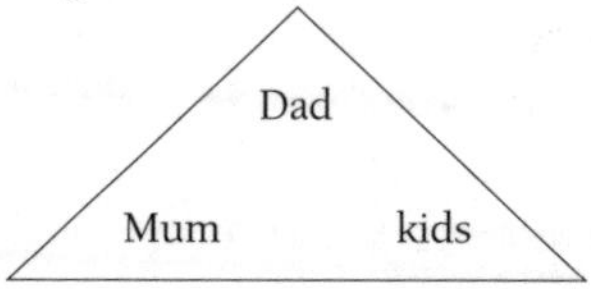

A PATRIARCHAL FAMILY

It can look very complicated:

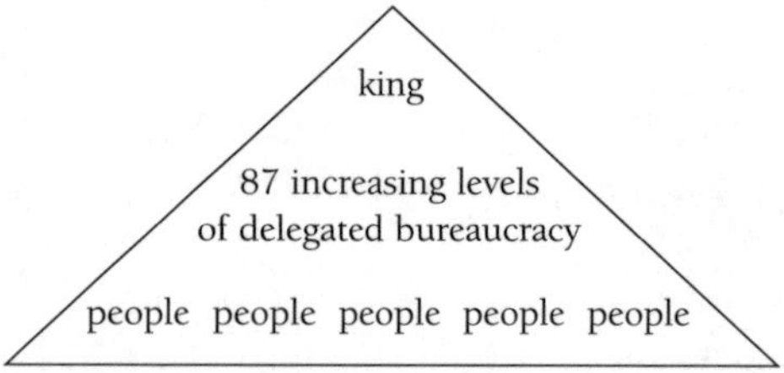

A KINGDOM

But whether it is simple or complex, whether it contains only one level of authority or hundreds, the shape is the same. There is only room for one person at the top and the shape of the top defines the shape of the whole, which makes it a 'top-down' structure.

We can find this sort of leadership configuration in every kind of culture. Whether we examine the government of the most powerful nation in the world or the leadership of the simplest, most isolated tribe in a rainforest clearing, a common structure can be found: a pyramid. Although different in scale, the leadership style is recognizable, and any criticisms will tend to stem from the fact that the person at the top is disliked for exercising authority in a cruel, totalitarian way, or that the way in which they got to the top is disliked as it wasn't by fair or democratic means.

In the Bible, a similar leadership pyramid is clearly evident. In the early days of the patriarchs, Abraham and his descendants (Isaac, Jacob and so on) occupied the top spot (Genesis 12—50). Their word was law and their decisions were final. From the time of Moses onwards (Exodus), the leadership of the emerging nation shifted to the prophet. Moving on to the period of the Judges, the prophet remained at the top of the leadership pyramid, but when there was a war an individual (a judge) was chosen to lead the people militarily for a season. Interestingly, it was the people who became disgruntled with this arrangement and wanted a permanent king (1 Samuel 8). From the time of the first king, Saul (1 Samuel 10), there was an interesting and unusual development: the nation had a king, but the prophet remained. In terms of leadership, Israel looked something like this:

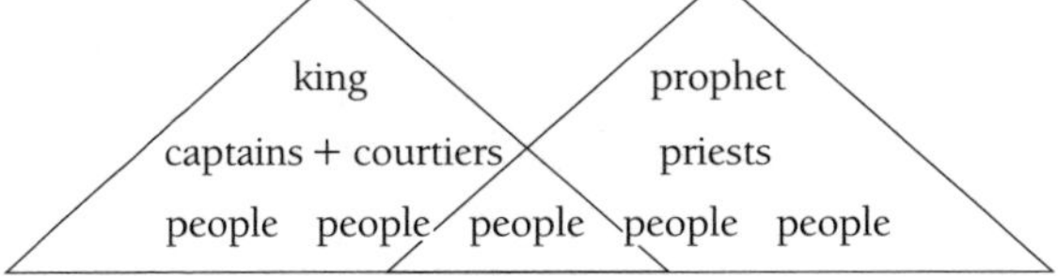

It was the king (with his captains and courtiers) who administered law and justice, engaged in international treaties and led the army. It was the prophet who advised on the law, considered the state of the nation and commented on the priesthood. In a secular nation, this twin-peaked leadership would spell disaster because there are two top spots. In Israel, it proved difficult because the prophet and the king were often at loggerheads (for example, Elijah and Ahab: see 1 Kings 17 onwards), but the structure worked because the king, the prophet and the people all understood that their leadership structure in fact had only one peak, not two. In their understanding, it looked like this:

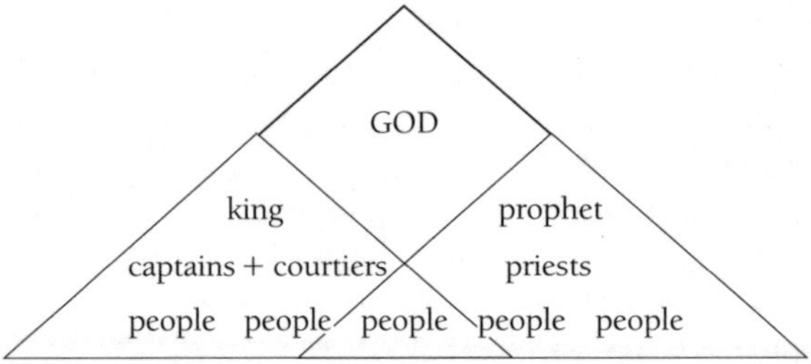

Neither the king nor the prophet was in charge; God was in charge. It was God who appointed and anointed both the prophet and the king, and they were equally responsible to God for their public roles and private lives. Therefore, the king was not allowed to behave as his kingly neighbours behaved, breaking the law when it suited him (2 Samuel 12:1–15), counting the nation as if he owned it (2 Samuel 24:1–25) or choosing his own religion (1 Kings 12:25–31). The bottom line was that if the leader behaved badly, he could be removed (1 Samuel 15:10—16:13), and the worst crime he could commit was to ignore God. Arguably, King David's behaviour was worse than King Saul's, but the difference between them was that David always repented.

So, whether looking back into history or across the world today, to religion or to secular practice, pyramid leadership is seen. Common wisdom says that the best possible person for the top job should be found, on the basis that if they are a good leader, then the whole pyramid benefits; if they are bad, then everyone else suffers. Therefore, in biblical terms, when there is a David (1 and 2 Samuel), a Solomon (1 Kings 1—11) or a Josiah (2 Kings 22—23) on the throne, the people experience a golden age; when there is an Ahab

(1 Kings 16—22) or a Herod (Matthew 2), then life is awful. This highlights the shortcomings of pyramid leadership, because in the whole history of the Hebrew people there was only ever one David, one Solomon and one Josiah.

THE WORDS OF JESUS

Jesus called them together and said, 'You know that the rulers of the Gentiles lord it over them, and their high officials exercise authority over them. Not so with you. Instead, whoever wants to become great among you must be your servant, and whoever wants to be first must be your slave—just as the Son of Man did not come to be served, but to serve, and to give his life as a ransom for many.'

MATTHEW 20:25–28

According to Jesus, his disciples should exercise leadership in a different way. This raises a few questions, the first of which is, 'Jesus says that his disciples should not follow the pattern of the Gentiles, so does he mean that they should follow the pattern of the religious leaders of his day?' Given that the leadership structure of the priesthood—the Pharisees, Sadducees and so forth—was identical to that of the Roman empire (a pyramid), this would be a baffling statement, especially considering Jesus' opinion of the religious leaders of his people. He regarded them as hypocrites (Matthew 6:5–6), unclean sinners (15:10–14), bad yeast (16:5–6), thieves (21:12–17), blind guides who refused to enter the kingdom of God themselves and locked the door for others (23:13–14), and that's taking his comments from just one Gospel. Although Jesus accepted the leadership pyramid (Matthew 23:1–3) his opinion of the king was low (Luke 13:31–32) and his opinion of religious leaders was even lower (Matthew 23:27–28, 33). Therefore, it's pretty unlikely that Jesus is commending the religious structure of his day as a pattern for his disciples.

Perhaps, then, Jesus' focus is on his disciples as servants. Perhaps he means, 'Keep the structure, but turn it upside down.' After all, servants are at the bottom of the pyramid, so if leaders are to serve, then this means turning the pyramid upside down—doesn't it? The problem with this thinking is the assumption that the culture of Jesus' day resembles our contemporary culture (in which servants are at the bottom of the social pile and there is little differentiation between 'servant' and 'wage-slave'). In fact, in Jesus' time, aristocrats were at the top (no change there!), merchants were the next level down, servants were next—but below them were labourers, then slaves and, at the very bottom, those who because of an illness (lepers, for example) were outside society altogether. Servants were in the middle of society and, to make things even more complicated, their status depended upon whom they served. Thus, the king's servants occupied a very high status indeed and the chief servant of an important man had enormous influence (Luke 16:1–9).

So if Jesus doesn't mean his disciples to be like the religious leaders of his day, and if he doesn't intend the pyramid to be turned upside down, what *does* he mean? The clue is in Matthew 23:8–11: 'But you are not to be called "Rabbi", for you have only one Master and you are all brothers. And do not call anyone on earth "father", for you have one Father, and he is in heaven. Nor are you to be called "teacher", for you have one Teacher, the Christ. The greatest among you will be your servant.' In this passage, Jesus points to the existing pyramidal structure of his day, where rabbis, teachers and fathers held authority. In each case, he reminds his disciples of the Old Testament model in which *God* was at the top of the pyramid. Servants and slaves were in the middle, so Jesus is saying, 'You should never occupy the top spot, because that belongs to God!' What this kind of leadership might look like in practice will be explored in subsequent chapters.

CHRISTIAN PYRAMIDS

The history of Christian leadership is a history of pyramid leadership. More specifically, it has tended to take the Old Testament model of leadership and align itself with the state in a recognizable double-peak formation. From this position it has sought to point the monarch towards God as his or her authority. Some Christian thinkers deplore this concept of the 'established' church and lay all the problems of church corruption at the door of the Emperor Constantine (who died in AD377). They believe that when Christianity moved from opposition to government, it lost its spiritual edge. This view, however, ignores the missionary thrust of the church since the time of Constantine. Whether we look at Augustine (who brought Christianity to Kent and died in AD430), Birinus (who ministered in the Thames valley and died in AD650) or more contemporary missionaries, their mode of operation was the same. In a society that operated pyramid leadership, if the person at the top was converted to Christianity, then the rest of the people would follow. Therefore, when missionaries landed on the shores of a new country, they sought as a first priority to make contact with the king or queen. Because of this initial relationship, the Christian church in each successfully converted country tended to take its place within the shape of leadership that was in operation through that state when the first missionaries arrived. So the pyramid continued, but with an additional Christian voice.

In contemporary Britain, two elements are at work. On the one hand, the established church is losing power, and on the other, the disestablished churches and those who hold other faiths are increasingly sharing the religious voice of the nation. This makes the present national structure much more complex: it is no longer Church and State with their twin peaks; it is now multicultural, multireligious and multipeaked. For Christians to behave as if one Christian denomination can provide the only religious peak is now untenable.

Leaving aside the national leadership of the church, however, and turning our attention to the leadership of the local church, an unsettling pattern begins to emerge. Increasingly, we find ourselves with leadership structures that no longer fit our culture, which drain us rather than empower us. We also find that whether we are part of the established church or not, whether our church is denominational or non-denominational, whether we are Christians or members of another religion, our leadership pyramid looks pretty much the same as everyone else's. So either leadership, by definition, has to be done the pyramidal way (in which case, what relevance do the words of Jesus in Matthew 20:25–28 have to the contemporary church?) or something is missing—and that 'something' is likely to be Collaborative Ministry.

Part One

A STRUCTURAL SURVEY

Chapter 2

GOING OUT AND BUILDING UP

The heartbeat of the Christian church is worship, but from the start it has been an evangelistic organization. The message that was first preached in Jerusalem continues to be preached to all nations (Luke 24:47) with the expectation that those who believe it will become disciples themselves, being baptized as a sign of their faith and learning obedience to God (Matthew 28:19–20). Thus, the church was launched with a twofold task;

1 **Going out:** This aspect of the task is seen in the missionary journeys of Paul, in the missionary activities of Christians through time and across the world, and in our own attempts to tell of what we know in our own neighbourhood.
2 **Building up:** Those who find faith join their local church, where they learn how to be Christian disciples.

Arguably, the task is threefold because it also includes the care of the needy in both the church and society. Certainly, in the history of the church, Christians have been at the forefront of meeting need through medicine, education, social welfare and direct financial aid. As Jesus said, there is never a shortage of people who need help (Matthew 26:11). Whether the church has a twofold, threefold (or more-fold) task is not the subject of this book, however. For the sake of simplicity, the pattern of the twofold task given by Jesus will be retained on the assumption that pastoral care is included in both going out and building up. Having said that, there is a balance between going out and building up, and the question is: how can the church get this balance right?

Looking at the New Testament, two answers emerge. First, there is a recognition that different Christians have different gifts. In Romans 12:6–8, for example, there is an expectation that some will be primarily 'givers of the message' (those who go out) while others will be primarily 'teachers and encouragers' (those who build up). If the church is healthy, then there will be a variety of God-given gifts being exercised for the benefit of the whole. Second, there is a recognition that those who become members will, in their turn, receive God-given gifts to contribute to the twofold task (1 Corinthians 12:7). There is an expectation that even when gifts differ, the task is corporate and all will contribute. To put it another way, fundamentally, ministry is collaborative.

The practical problem is this: how should this multiplicity of ministry be organized?

FOUR FAMILIAR PASSAGES

When it comes to the organization of the church, four Bible passages are commonly considered: Exodus 18:13–26; the book of Nehemiah; Luke 10:1–20; and Acts 6:1–7.

Exodus 18:13–26

Here, Moses (at the apex of pyramid leadership) is struggling to fulfil his duties. Jethro, his father-in-law, tells him to appoint men to preside over 'thousands, hundreds, fifties and tens' (v. 21). Thus, simple disputes will be settled quickly by the lower-level appointees, while more complex issues will rise up through the pyramid. On the way up, many of these issues will also be sorted out by the higher-level appointees and Moses himself will deal only with the thorniest problems. In this passage, Moses delegates to leaders on the basis of their personal faith, capability, trustworthiness and honesty.

Once the system is set up, we hear little about it. In Exodus, the following chapters tell of the people's journey to Sinai, where Moses received the Ten Commandments. Interestingly, when Deuteronomy covers the same ground (Deuteronomy 5—10), it tells of the people's disobedience and lack of faith. This rather begs the questions, 'So where were the leaders of the thousands, hundreds, fifties and tens? Shouldn't at least some of them have spoken up in protest?' This is a reminder that setting up an organization is not the same thing as managing it! With pyramid leadership in particular, once the levels are set up, they require constant attention by the person at the top. This is because delegation is a combination of allocation and entrustment. What is allocated needs checking; what is entrusted needs monitoring because those who share the top man's load do just that—share it. They assist him in his task and shoulder a degree of his responsibility, but the task, and the responsibility, remain his.

Nehemiah

Over the past two decades, the book of Nehemiah has been widely used as a metaphorical pattern for building up the church. In the early chapters, Nehemiah shows great faith in God (and considerable personal courage) as he brings to the attention of the Persian Emperor Artaxerxes the plight of his homeland. With letters of authority in hand, Nehemiah returns to Jerusalem. He organizes the people by giving each family responsibility for rebuilding its own section of the city wall and, against local opposition, he succeeds.

It's a wonderful story of bravery, faith, wisdom and barefaced cheek. It also (to the delight of those who believe that the church should remain in partnership with the state) underlines how important it is to be backed by an empire. At the end of the day, though, it describes how to build a city wall, not how to build a church. The aim of Nehemiah was to make Jerusalem safe from the surrounding kings, in the hope that when the city was rebuilt his nation might arise once more, and this is exactly what happened.

What is often forgotten is that as well as rebuilding Jerusalem, Nehemiah rebuilt temple worship, the priesthood, the temple guard, the sabbath, tithes and a multiplicity of regulations. Subsequent generations refined his new-build to the point where, in the Gospels, Jesus criticizes the religious leaders of his day for being long on rules and short on spirit. Where did this begin? With Nehemiah. Very possibly, those who take the 'Nehemiah pattern' and apply it to the church today will discover that future generations refine it to the point where church members can't get out—and seekers can't get in.

Luke 10:1–20

In this passage, Jesus sends 72 disciples ahead of him to heal the sick and to proclaim that the kingdom is near. This passage is about 'going out', and there are three 'rules' in operation:

1 The 72 are sent out in pairs. The early church seems to follow this same pattern—for example, when Paul and Barnabas are sent as missionaries (Acts 13:2–3).
2 They are told to stay where they are welcomed and to leave when they are not.
3 Their proclamation ('The kingdom is near') is complemented and confirmed by their actions (healing).

This passage is often cited as a pattern for building up the church because of 'rule 1'. It is certainly true that going-out activity, like building-up activity, was corporate. There was little in the New Testament experience that was individual, apart from the personal decision of faith (Acts 2:38). Prayer was corporate (for example, the 'you' in Matthew 6:5 is plural: it means 'When you [lot] pray [together])' and was done with others (Acts 4:24); possessions were held in common (Acts 2:44) and the expectation was that when Christians met together, shared together and went out in evangelistic ministry together, then the risen Christ was present (Matthew 18:20; 28:20). Having said that, though, the sending out of the 72 does not properly belong to the 'building up' part of the twofold task (and, primarily, this book focuses on this second aspect). The passage is mentioned here only to make that point clear.

Acts 6:1–7

At first glance, this New Testament passage looks very similar to Exodus 18. The apostles, like Moses, are facing disputes among their people and don't have the time to give their personal attention to sorting out the difficulties. Also, as in the 'Moses solution', leaders are appointed to deal with the problems (seven leaders on this occasion) and they are chosen on the basis of their spirituality and wisdom. Here, however, the similarity stops, because there are three major differences.

First, Moses chose his leaders (and they answered to him), but the seven were chosen by the whole church (and were answerable to them). Second, the apostles were not involved in the choice or in the management of the seven; they gave their time to prayer and to preaching (going out). Third, when the seven were chosen, the apostles laid hands on them and prayed for them, and the seven got on with the job. The apostles also got on with theirs, with the result that even more people joined the church (v. 7).

These differences point up an overlooked fact. In the Old Testament, kings and prophets might receive the Holy Spirit of God for their task, but the general populace did not. In the New Testament, the prophecy of Joel (2:28–29) had become a reality and the Holy Spirit was received by everyone. Therefore, the church was left to elect the seven and, when elected, the seven were entrusted with the whole task. Why? Because in the Old Testament example, Moses was in charge; in this New Testament passage, the Holy Spirit was in charge.

THE FOUR PASSAGES INTERPRETED

Most usually, these four Bible passages are related directly to the local church. Exodus 18, for example, might be used as a leadership pattern for both small and large churches. The local minister will be assigned the role of Moses, while the varying levels of local leaders will be identified as leaders of tens, fifties, hundreds and even thousands. There is a problem with using the Bible in this way, however. Exodus 18 describes a nation, not a local community. If, for example, this passage is applied to a local situation in the Church of England, the role of Moses should be assigned to the Archbishop of Canterbury, the leaders of thousands would be bishops, vicars would be the leaders of hundreds, with the leaders of fifties and tens identified as leaders within the local church. The problem for the local church is that Exodus describes how Moses functioned within the structure but has little, if anything, practical to say to the leaders of the hundreds. Perhaps the only real lesson of this passage is one of humility: church ministers, you are not Moses! Learn your place!

Similarly, when Nehemiah is used as a parable of leadership, scripture is stretched. Why go searching for a parable when the Bible provides direct teaching and theology elsewhere? The sad answer is that most of us are tempted to look for passages that bolster our view of leadership while ignoring those that challenge it. Both Exodus 18 and the book of Nehemiah allow us to retain our familiar pyramid leadership, where the focus is on good (and godly) delegation to good (and godly) delegates.

Our use of the Bible is exposed by our treatment of Acts 6. If this passage is used in conjunction with Exodus and Nehemiah, then we have either read it selectively or failed to understand it. Acts 6 does not describe delegation but collaboration, and the practical theology of it concerns each person (whether they are an apostle, one of the seven, or 'just' a church member), being equally filled with the Holy Spirit. The church leadership structure described in Acts is nothing like the Old Testament pattern. The apostles are not leaders in the same way that Moses or Nehemiah were leaders, because the Holy Spirit is in charge not only of them, but also of those whom they lead. This issue (and the implications of it) is considered in more depth in Part Two.

COMMUNITY VERSUS INDIVIDUALISM

The cultures described in both the Old and New Testaments were community-minded, whereas our contemporary culture is individualistic. Whether we regard this shift as good or bad will depend on our point of view, but the truth is that there are advantages and disadvantages to both cultural attitudes. Community-minded societies are strong on pastoral care, but individuals who do not 'fit in' are often repressed or driven away. Individualistic societies are strong on personal fulfilment, but those who 'can't cut it' are often ignored or despised. In the final analysis, neither is perfect—which should not surprise Christian people, believing as we do that the human race is fallen. Understanding the culture in which we live is important, though, if the church is to 'go out' and 'build up' appropriately.

When the focus is on leadership structures, it's helpful to recognize that New Testament religious leadership does not simply continue from where the Old Testament leaves it. Before the coming of Christ, the culture of the Hebrew people was focused on the community, but leadership was individualistic and highly autocratic. This harmonized with the Old Testament reality that only certain key leaders were empowered with the Spirit of God. After the resurrection of Christ, however, it was not only the people who behaved as a community; so did the leaders. Again, this harmonized with their experience that the Holy Spirit empowered them all. In our contemporary culture, Christians are coming to terms with society's shift to individualism, while continuing to uphold the values of 'community' within the church. The question is: when we think about leadership structures that encourage the 'going out' and 'building up' aspects of the church's ministry, why do we revert to an individualistic approach to leadership which is more in tune with the Old Testament than with the New?

SOME QUESTIONS TO THINK ABOUT

- 'Going out' is like the church breathing out, while 'building up' can be compared to the church breathing in. What happens if the church only does one or the other?
- In what ways is the experience of Moses and the Hebrews relevant to church life in the third millennium?
- Can the appointment of the seven (in Acts) be related to our own church? Is this kind of pattern used when appointing people to leadership?

Chapter 3

LOOKING AT LEADERSHIP

Let's consider the following diagram of traditional church leadership, which will probably be familiar to most people:

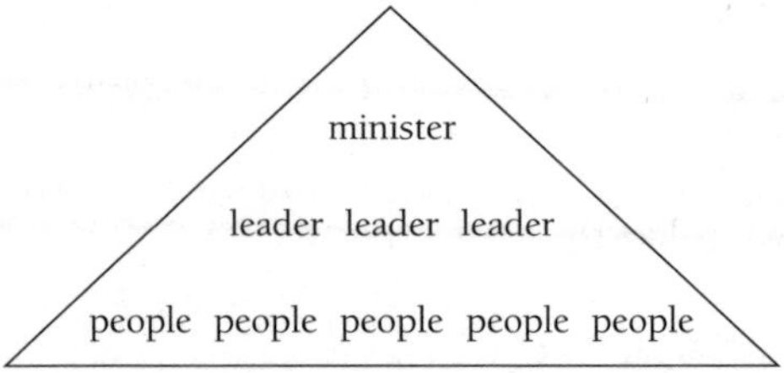

The chain of command is identical to the armed forces, business, government, the local community and traditional family life. It requires levels of leadership with one person at the top (the king, the managing director, the father, the minister), assistant leaders to whom the top person relates, and people to whom, in turn, these leaders relate as they implement laws, decisions and so forth. Every human being is familiar with the leadership pyramid. Most of us are introduced to it early in life, perhaps by becoming 'pencil monitor' (or such like) in primary school and being elevated above our peers to occupy a leadership space between the teacher and the class. It is our first taste of both responsibility and power. Many people make 'the top' their goal in life; to be the one who gives the orders is perceived as success and is rewarded accordingly.

We are probably also familiar with this style of leadership in our churches. For example, when the minister is expected to be the person who has vision (or receives vision), the church is acknowledging that he is the pinnacle person. Similarly, when one minister is appointed to lead four, six or even ten churches, there is an implicit admission that each church must have a 'top man'. In both examples, no one else in the church is regarded as capable of leading in this way; the pinnacle is one person wide—and that person is the minister.

There are a number of problems with pyramids, however.

- The stability of the structure depends upon having lots of people at the bottom. If there are only a few, the structure becomes more like a column, with the risk that it will fall over.
- The minister may be inappropriately revered. This becomes a problem if his thoughts and judgments on every issue are then given too much weight. If he is wise, humble and godly, all may be well; if he is foolish, proud and self-seeking, there may be enormous problems.
- If he is inappropriately revered, the minister becomes isolated. He may feel that he cannot show weakness, ignorance or character flaws. To a small or large extent, he may maintain an outward show.
- Assistant leaders emulate their minister. The higher they rise in the church, the more revered and isolated they tend to become themselves.
- The church has a clear hierarchy, which, for all the wrong reasons, may attract all the wrong people towards leadership.
- It may create a culture of unhelpful dependency, typified by the member who is highly competent at work but becomes a 'passenger' in church.
- It tends to mitigate against growth because it limits the leadership: in our individualistic culture, members expect to relate individually to the main leader, not primarily to the church community. Therefore, if there is only one 'top man', the church can only grow to a certain number of members.
- When the minister leaves, retires or dies, everything changes, because even in a well-delegated church, the minister tends to retain power.

Pyramid leadership is fraught with pitfalls. The fact that a particular church is currently 'going well' will not remove the problems. Even in a big, successful church, a minister who operates pyramid leadership will tend to be isolated, and the people of that church may well have an unrealistic view of him while being dependent on him. The minister may be responsible for a great work of growth while at the same time sowing the seeds of destruction for his successor.

It is possible, however, for a minister to lead a pyramid well.

GOOD PYRAMID LEADERSHIP

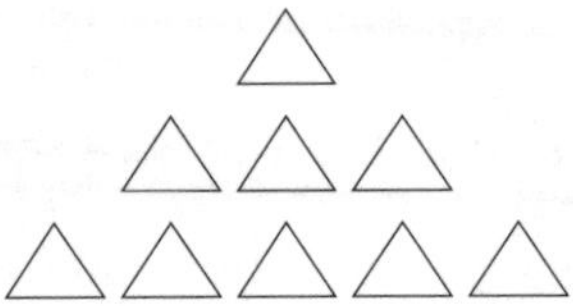

It is rightly said that the minister is often 'the stopper in the bottle' of a church. When pyramid leadership is done well, it's always because the minister has learned how to be a 'valve'. He allows ideas, initiatives and so on not only to come to him but through him. Often, this leads to a circulation of initiatives as the minister receives them and then feeds them back to one of his leaders. In this model of church, some leaders become heads of departments, so there is someone in charge of administration, youth work, music, evangelism, pastoral care and so forth. At the top of the top pyramid is the minister; at the bottom of the top pyramid are the heads of department. They then, in their turn, are at the top of the next row of pyramids, and the leaders who work in their departments form the bottom layer of the middle pyramids. These leaders then occupy the top of the next pyramid, working with the people.

In large churches, these head-of-department roles can be full-time, paid posts, so each 'staff member' relates primarily to the minister (above them) and to volunteer leaders (below them) who, in their turn, relate to 'the people'. This structure is a micro-version of the macro-version of traditional denominations. The minister of this kind of church is, then, as it were, exercising a 'micro-episcopal' role.

In secular society and the business world, pyramid leadership works well because the goals are simple. In a trading company, for example, the main aim of the organization might be to make money. In a government, the main aim may be to steward power in order to govern. Pyramid leadership is very good at providing individuals with the opportunity to pursue personal wealth and power. It also lends itself to achieving ends while not being particular about the means, and many people may fall as casualties to pay for the upward mobility of the few. The harsh truth is that pyramid leadership succeeds even when those at the top care nothing for those at the bottom. To win a war, the monarch needs cannon fodder.

This brings us to the question of power, who should hold it, and how. In the Old Testament (as noted in Chapter 1), neither the king nor the prophet held ultimate power; both were subject to God (and to the scrutiny of each other). This theology is endorsed by Paul in Romans 13:1–5. Here, he regards the Roman authorities as occupying the same 'space' between God and the people as an Old Testament king. Implicit in his thinking is not only the stated need for the people to be obedient to this authority but also the recognition that secular authorities are accountable to God. So what is an appropriate way to handle the authority delegated by God?

What if those people who occupy the base of the pyramid are important? What if the whole structure is actually set up for the benefit of those who occupy the lowest place? Is it possible for those who occupy the pinnacle to care about those at the bottom? As far as the church is concerned, this is the key question, because without the people there is no church! Therefore, the church (in its building-up aspect) is fundamentally there to serve its people in the same way that it exists for the benefit of non-members (in its going-out aspect).

Jesus said, 'You know that the rulers of the Gentiles lord it over them, and their high officials exercise authority over them. Not so with you' (Matthew 20:25–26a). Thus, we have to ask: can a church that behaves in pyramidal fashion fulfil its remit? If Jesus is to be believed, then the answer must be 'No'. Is there an alternative, though? Although some ministers are fiercely holding on to 'their ministry', determined to keep it out of the clutches of everyone else, reality is knocking on even the most barred and bolted doors. In some parts of the church, two facts—shrinking congregations and fewer 'professional' leaders—are concentrating the minds of many. In other parts of the church, success stories are keenly sought after in the hope that a blueprint may be found for success everywhere. In every part of the church, Christians are being forced to rethink ministry, and there are three key questions involved.

The first question

In a church with 100 members, is it the job of the minister to build up those 100 members (and also his job to go out to the 8000 people in his parish/area/town), or is it the job of those 101 members (the 100 plus the minister) to build one another up and go out to the 8000 together? Most churches these days will answer 'Yes' to the second half of this question: the minister and church members will therefore wish to collaborate in some way in order to achieve their mutual task.

The second question

In a church of 1000 members, does the same pattern apply? From observation, the answer would seem to be 'No'. In a large church, there will probably be several keen evangelists who major on 'going-out' activities; there may even be a staff member paid to lead this ministry. The minister, however, tends to function in a highly traditional role, spending his time building up (or managing) the church. Many members involved in active church work will have a sense of working with the minister even though they never contribute directly to his tasks (or he to theirs), which points to his role as a figurehead.

The third question

If collaboration means working together, why is it elusive? Leaving aside the matter of churches that believe delegation to be collaboration (and therefore ignore both the theology and practice of CM), there is a church size issue here. Small churches tend to think that they do not have enough members to organize a collaborative structure. They presume that what is needed is departments and leaders, and that they need more members before they can make any changes. Large churches, on the other hand, tend to think that it would be much easier to create a collaborative structure if the church was smaller because the present leadership structure is complex and the thought of changing it is daunting. In both small and large churches, assistant leaders are hard to find and a few overworked people seem to do everything while the majority look on with either approval or criticism. Whether we belong to a small church or a large church, we may find ourselves looking around and asking, 'Is this what Jesus wants church to be like?'

ON THE BUSES

If we think of the church in terms of transport (which is not stretching the imagination too far, as we are probably familiar with the idea of Christians being 'a pilgrim people'), it helps to recognize that some church members have absolutely no desire at all to share the driving (ministry). For them, it is enough to be a passenger. They are happy to pay for their ticket, enjoy the ride, point out the flaws in the route and criticize the driver (the minister). Similarly, there are others whose main aim is to receive personal attention from the driver, and they don't care if the bus (the church) has to park in a layby while their needs take up the driver's time. As far as they are concerned, the church exists for their personal benefit.

Also, there are a number of drivers who have no desire to share their work. They feel that there is only room for one driver and certain assistants. If there were any more, it would spoil the organization. In fact, as only a finite number of assistants are needed, it's possible for that minister to pick only the most acceptable people (in other words, those who agree with him on most issues).

In our changing and challenging culture, these attitudes are a cause of increasing frustration. Overworked core leaders may be fed up with tolerating increasing numbers of passengers while, at the same time, church members, feeling excluded by a defensive leadership, are likely to demand inclusion. If, however, these frustrations lead us to turn to management techniques, one frustration will probably be substituted for another. Some churches are already on their second, third or fourth 'let's do church *this* way!' programme and yet nothing very significant seems to change. The fact is that if any church fails to grapple with its theology of leadership, then the new way of organizing the church will, in reality, look pretty much the same as the style of leadership that was abandoned!

The idea of CM has been bubbling around for a long time, even though it has been called 'enabling', 'every-member ministry', or the 'priesthood of all believers' (each of which is an attempt to summarize the teaching found in 1 Peter 2 and Hebrews 2—8). So, when considering our own churches (whatever their size or denomination), it's worth asking, 'Is this what "enabled" or "shared" or "every member" ministry looks like?' or, 'In what sense is this a priesthood of us all?' Another way of looking at the same issue is to recognize that the minister will be able to answer the following question very easily: 'What exactly is my ministry here?' At the same time, it may be very hard for church members to answer the same question—unless they answer, 'That's easy. I'm not the minister so I don't have a ministry!' If, however, the church is truly a priesthood of all believers, where every member has a ministry, then every person in the church should be able to answer the question with the same conviction as their minister.

Over the last 20 years there has been a growing recognition that pyramidal leadership is no longer appropriate. To facilitate change, two significant models of leadership have been widely adopted. Let's consider them now.

SERVANT LEADERSHIP

This style of leadership has been taught since the late 1980s. It seeks to take seriously the 'servant' model from scripture, address the changing nature of society and look outwards. It states that the inverted triangle of service can grow ever larger as the church serves the community. The theory is this: the minister serves the leaders, the leaders serve the church members and the church members serve their friends, neighbours and community. As everyone looks outwards, it is possible for the church to serve the whole world.

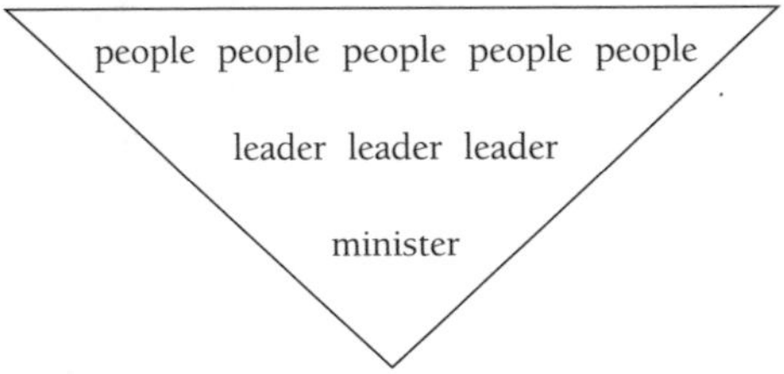

This model has been embraced by many who find it attractive and understandable because it involves little change. It's the model of leadership we are used to (a pyramid)—it's just the other way up.

All that is required is that we do what we've always done: we just think differently about what we're doing and how we do it.

In practice, this style of leadership is not, in fact, servant leadership. First, as we have already seen in Chapter 1, the servant in New Testament culture was not at the bottom of society's pile but somewhere in the middle. To equate the minister with a servant and just turn the traditional model upside down is to do gymnastics with the words of Jesus. Second, this model is actually exactly what it looks like—an inverted pyramid. This is an inherently unstable structure because:

- The stability of the structure and the direction of the organization depends upon one person.
- The minister is still revered, but not for his 'loftiness'. Instead, his hard work and dedication are valued—which is a recipe for personal burn-out.
- The minister is probably still isolated, but now, instead of being able to direct other leaders, he must serve them.

Sooner or later, the pyramid will either topple over or squash the minister. In reality, most 'servant leaders' operate pyramid leadership. The terminology may be about 'service' but the reality is that they are firmly in charge. Church members and leaders who are (according to the model) above them are actually below them. The church may be drawn as an inverted pyramid on paper, but in reality it operates traditionally with the minister at the top. Those who genuinely try to serve according to this model set themselves up for failure because, ultimately, no one has the personal strength to carry such a structure.

Many recent books on Christian leadership have been written because the authors are concerned about ministerial burn-out. It would be interesting to survey churches where the minister has burnt out and see how many of them tried to operate servant leadership.

THE JESUS MODEL

This style of leadership describes Jesus in the middle surrounded by his disciples.

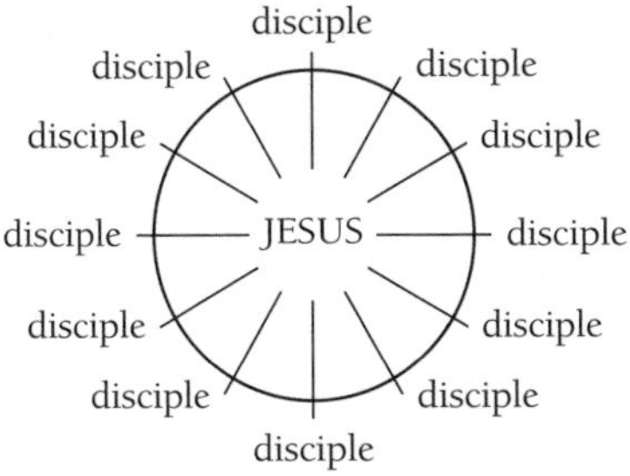

As a model of leadership, this is widely accepted because the Gospels make it clear that Jesus did indeed have this sort of relationship with his disciples. However, this structure is nothing new. Actually, it's a pyramid (or cone) viewed from above!

In the early church, the same pattern continues; it does not change. For example, thinking of Paul in terms of Christian leadership, he worked with a variety of people, such as Barnabas, John Mark, Silas, Timothy, Priscilla and Aquila (Acts 13:2, 13; 15:40; 16:1–2; 18:18) and engaged in leadership with the other apostles (Acts 15:1–21; 21:17–26). Paul had strongly held opinions on various subjects, but it's a struggle to work out where Paul sat in a pyramid of power. He clearly didn't occupy the top spot: if anything, he seems to have occupied the position of a disciple who looks to Jesus. So in the early church, who occupied the pinnacle?

Actually, trying to put Peter or James or Mark (or anyone) in the top spot does not accord with the book of Acts or with the epistles. The truth is that none of these early 'ministers' sought to replace Jesus. Each apostle looked to the risen and ascended Christ as the one pinnacle leader, and so did every other believer. This was their understanding in Acts 6, when the seven 'helpers' were appointed. They were not assistant pyramidal leaders who were appointed and managed by the apostles. They were appointed as fellow assistant leaders by the church and were anointed for the task by the Holy Spirit (which is why the apostles lay hands on them in verse 6). They were answerable to Christ, not to the apostles (which is why the apostles got on with their own task and left the seven to get on with theirs). This same attitude is seen when Paul and Barnabas are sent off in mission (Acts 13:1–3).

What we see is disciples engaging with tasks, empowered by the Holy Spirit and answerable to Jesus Christ. What we never see is layers of carefully defined leadership. This is because these people are operating a new system that fulfils Jesus' promise in Matthew 20:25–28. They are taking the roles of servant according to the culture of the day: they are the middle men between God and people but their position is defined by task, not authority. They are all equally dependent upon the living God, and the differences between them are not defined on the basis of 'who's in charge of whom' but on the basis of whom the Holy Spirit has anointed to do what.

When Jesus is at the centre of this model of leadership, he is exactly where he should be. The problem with the 'Jesus style' comes when we remove Jesus from the centre, replace him with the minister of the local church—and then remove the disciples and replace them with church leaders. In this version of the 'Jesus style' of leadership, Jesus himself has disappeared. In fact, of course, the minister is a disciple like any other and belongs in a 'disciple' position, not in the 'Jesus' position. If Jesus is replaced with the minister, then the church is proclaiming, in effect, that Jesus died on the cross but never rose from the dead. In practical terms, the result is that Jesus is no longer at the centre (or at the top of the pyramid); the minister has replaced him.

DOES IT MATTER?

Here we come to the crux of the matter. In society, pyramidal leadership tends to benefit the few at the expense of the many. Why would we think that the same structure will produce different results in the church? Let's over-exaggerate for effect:

- In a settled, class-conscious culture, pyramidal leadership allows a few people to keep the majority in line. The ordinary person, regardless of ability or calling, will never be accepted into the higher echelons and the hierarchy can behave abominably if they want to because they control society, opinion and decision-making.
- In a mobile, classless culture, pyramidal leadership creates a platform from which pinnacle people may plummet. Because ordinary people now affiliate to individuals rather than to communities (where it doesn't matter so much who is at the top, as long as they are competent), when a minister leaves and a new one arrives, it can be a much bigger deal than it used to be. Even if the new minister is as able as the old one, the church may still fail because in a mobile, classless society a pyramid exists from day to day by the renewed commitment of its members. If they withdraw their good will, the person at the top begins to teeter (this issue is looked at in more detail in Chapter 4).

Of course, this is an over-exaggeration because whatever leadership structure a church operates, God tends to work with it. This is seen to be true in both the past and the present, as the lives of men, women and children are touched by God. Even where the church is responsible for the most appalling abuses, the grace of God still abounds (a fact established in the early church—for example, in Corinth). That said, neither of the two extremes above are conducive to the 'going out' and 'building up' ministry to which the people of God are called.

To put it bluntly, pyramidal church structures tend to militate against growth. In the first example (where the hierarchy determines the agenda), it's the personal growth of the individual that suffers, because the well-being of the individual is irrelevant to the success of the structure. The church then has a tendency to fail in its mission to build up its members appropriately. In the second example (where the hierarchy is expected to respond to a multiplicity of individual demands), it's the growth of the church in terms of congregational numbers that suffers, because too much energy is concentrated on providing for the needs of existing members. The church then has a tendency to fail in its mission to go out appropriately. Therefore, how we 'do church' is an important issue.

Whether our leadership structure is working well or failing miserably, leaving it alone is not an option. Jesus is very clear about this: healthy trees are pruned, and fruitless trees are removed (Luke 13:6–9; John 15:1–4). There is always a period of grace, but ultimately fruit is expected. If we are tempted to apply these parables only to individual lives and not to the church, then we should read Luke 3:8–9, where John the Baptist uses a similar image to speak of God's judgment upon the holy nation.

THE GRACE OF GOD

God takes account of our attitude to (and faith in) Christ before he considers what any of us can do for him (John 6:28–29). In biblical terms, this is an aspect of God's grace (Ephesians 2:4–5), and a Christian life is not so much judged by good works done as by the primary work of God in the Christian, which is expressed secondarily in good works that are then done (Ephesians 2:10). This means that God accepts and blesses any work undertaken in the right spirit. In a church that exercises good pyramid leadership, the prevailing attitude among church members will be, 'We want to help our minister in his ministry.' By God's grace, this attitude of humble service will be accepted and blessed. Similarly, in a church committed to servant leadership, the minister's attitude will be, 'I want to help the church members in their ministry', and this too will be accepted and blessed. God loves to bless (Ephesians 1:3) and, thankfully, he takes and uses our often pitiful attempts at service, fills them with his own Spirit and we give glory to God for the result! In other words, whether church leadership is organized well, badly, appropriately or inappropriately, if our motives are to serve God, there are usually godly results.

There is a counterbalance, however. As Paul points out in Ephesians 2:10, God expects to be in charge of what we do, and when the church exercises pyramid leadership (even when it is reinvented as 'servant leadership' or 'the Jesus model') we replace God with human beings.

In CM, the attitude of both the minister and church members will be, 'How can we minister together?' Built into the structure is the authority of God, the headship of Christ and the expectation that the Holy Spirit will both stimulate, and give gifts for, ministry. CM recognizes at an organizational level that without God, the church must fail.

BACK ON THE BUSES

Let's revisit the metaphor of transport to distinguish traditional hierarchical leadership (the pyramid) and good hierarchical leadership (the delegated pyramid) from CM. For many hundreds of years, our culture was stable and it was therefore unnecessary for the church to 'go' anywhere. During this period, churches were like big buses that had no route; they were 'parked' in every community and all that was required of most people was to 'get on'. The remit of the church was to baptize and confirm into membership, marry and bury parishioners while helping them to be good Christians along the way. A few people ministered to the many, and pyramid leadership underpinned the social status quo.

For about a hundred years now, society has been changing with escalating rapidity. It is no longer stable or static, and the church cannot survive when it is 'parked' because most people just ignore it. Initially, it was enough that existing passengers brought new passengers to the bus, but increasingly it became apparent that the bus would have to move. Delegation is akin to downsizing the original bus and adding a fleet of minibuses that drive in convoy with it. The minibuses still need the big bus because it defines the route, and without a strong leader driving the big bus (and keeping in close touch with the minibus drivers to make sure that they are where they should be), everyone gets lost.

CM gets rid of the big bus altogether. Instead of a convoy, the whole church is divided into areas of ministry that can be thought of as a variety of vehicles (some bigger, some smaller), and the destination is agreed. The route is left to each individual vehicle, and, with the proviso that each one keeps in touch with all the others, they set off. Everyone is regarded as a potential driver and it is left to each vehicle to decide who is going to drive and for how long. To think of CM as having leaders at every level is fundamentally to misunderstand the nature of collaboration. There are no 'levels' in CM, only 'areas of ministry', and these areas are not defined by either size or visibility. Leadership is distributed across the church, ministry is a response to the call of God, and the driving force behind the entire structure is the Holy Spirit.

SOME QUESTIONS TO THINK ABOUT

1 In our church, what is the ratio between drivers and passengers? Who is it that keeps it this way?
2 Do we operate (or have we operated) servant leadership? Does the minister seek to serve everyone… and is he surviving?
3 If we operate the Jesus model, and have replaced Jesus with our minister, how do we feel about this theology? How do we think Jesus feels about it?

Chapter 4

DELEGATION AND COLLABORATION

In recent years, Rothauge's[1] description of how churches of different sizes function has been widely used. He identifies four 'categories' of church:

- **The family church** (1–50 members) functions by the minister sharing a parental role with indigenous matriarchs and patriarchs.
- **The pastoral church** (50–150 members) functions by the minister assuming a central, pastoral role.
- **The programme church** (150–350 members) functions by the minister assuming a central, managerial role.
- **The corporation church** (350+ members) functions like a business with the minister assuming the role of the managing director.

Although some churches recognize (and think in terms of) the corporation church, others now replace it with **the Minster church** (350+ members with one large central church plus satellite congregations), which functions through the minister assuming a mini-episcopal role.

Originally, Rothauge identified these four categories of church in order to help congregations of every size to welcome and assimilate new members. He recognized that the congregational size of churches would be shaped by external forces (geographical location, local population, cultural expectations and so forth) as well as by internal factors (popularity of the minister, friendliness of the members and so forth). His expectation was that there would be churches of varying sizes serving different communities, and his thesis was that because each type of church functions differently, going out and building up should be appropriate to the resources and relationship dynamic of each one.

In current usage, these four categories tend to be used as more than descriptions of size, and are often presented as a blueprint for growth. The implication is, then, that every family church will one day become a corporation or Minster church. The focus often becomes the invisible barrier between the pastoral church and the programme church, because there is a tendency for churches to 'stick' at below 150 members (due to the reluctance of the minister to move into a managerial role, or the reluctance of church members to accept such a move).

Rothauge's categories are both accurate and helpful descriptions of leadership. They accord with a common experience of church and rightly point out a major problem—that it is not possible for more than 150 people to relate to the minister. Each of the four categories, however, presume both pyramidal leadership and one central church (the big bus). Therefore, while the four categories describe four sizes of pyramidal leadership, they do not engage with the central aspect of the leadership structure that is common to all four. The minister's role is described in classic pyramidal terms as he moves from being a parent to a pastor before becoming a manager and then a managing director (or mini-bishop). The movement is achieved by adding extra layers of delegated leadership at each point of change. This leaves us with certain difficulties:

- The premise of size: the assumption that it is both possible and desirable for every church to become a corporation or Minster church.
- The premise of centralism: the assumption that the minister remains in place but adds layers of delegated leadership, to which the congregation must relate.

- An inherited theology: the assumption that our theology of leadership is correct.

To sum up, this fourfold description of church is often applied in two specific ways. First, it is used to highlight a specific problem: how to grow every church in size to 350+ members. Second, it is used to focus on the necessity of changing the pattern of leadership when a church does grow (whatever its initial size, whether 50, 150 or even 350 members). In actual fact, Rothauge's description suggests that the leadership structure restricts not only the sub-150-member churches, but every church.

Pyramidal leadership tends to locate itself centrally because the central leader can only be in one place at a time. Therefore, the church tends to locate where it perceives the leadership to be. In practical terms, this usually means that if a church has a multiplicity of ministers, there will probably be a multiplicity of meeting places. If the church has one minister, there will probably be only one main building that is perceived by the church as the hub of activity. An example of this can be seen when new churches begin by meeting in a variety of locations and hiring a central venue for Sunday worship. After a time, there is a tendency to move to a permanent, central building. In part, this is a practical decision (because, after 15 years, everyone gets tired of setting out and removing furniture) but the shift also tends to indicate a particular attitude towards leadership. The move to a permanent building makes gathered worship easier but it also tends to centralize ministry (back on to the big, stationary bus).

Collaborative Ministry offers an alternative because it is a 'one-size-fits-all' pattern of leadership. It can be a way forward for small churches wrestling with failure, and also for large churches struggling with success. If CM is established in a small church, when the congregation grows, it is not necessary to change the style of leadership. Similarly, when a middle-sized church grows into a large church, CM can grow with it. It is also possible to foster CM in one limited area of church life (perhaps in a church where the complete replacement of pyramidal leadership at once is unacceptable) or even across a multicongregational or geographically wide area. Regardless of whether there is a large central building or not (a parked bus), ministry (the activity of the church) is spread across a variety of vehicles (areas of ministry), and the leadership structure remains the same whether there are six, 60 or 600 of them. CM is, to use contemporary jargon, future-proof!

DELEGATION AND COLLABORATION

Delegation and collaboration differ at a fundamental level because, in each system, final responsibility rests in a different place. Pyramidal leadership lends itself to delegation because, at each level, leaders accept direction from above and pass it on down. If there are problems, they are passed back up. If the structure is well delegated, ordinary decisions and problems will be dealt with somewhere in the middle of the structure, and only crises will go all the way to the top (the 'Moses pattern' of Exodus 18). If the structure is poorly delegated, the pinnacle person will try to make every decision and solve every problem alone. However well or badly the structure is delegated, the communications flow is the same: orders go down and responsibility goes back up, and ultimately the buck stops with the person at the top. In a collaborative structure, the buck is interchangeable. A simple way to think about this is to imagine a number of churches working together, like this:

These churches might be sister churches in the same denomination or in an ecumenical covenant, or working together informally in a defined geographical area. Each one is a pyramid in its own right and each has its own minister, but they choose to work together, perhaps on a particular project. The question is: how will the six churches work together when there are six ministers? Who is in charge? There are two solutions.

- Either, they elect one of the six to act as 'minister in chief' and create a pyramidal structure where he co-ordinates different aspects of the work that is delegated to others
- Or, they collaborate together, each taking responsibility for a different aspect of the project. The structure is then similar to a secular business partnership, because the ministers are collaborating (CL).

In the first approach, if the project fails, then the buck will stop with the minister-in-chief. In the second approach, the buck stops with the person in charge of the 'failed bit'. In the first way of working, responsibility is centralized; in the second, it is shared—among the ministers at least.

COLLABORATION IN THE LOCAL CHURCH

Let's transpose the same diagram into one local church. Instead of six churches, let's say that there are six areas of ministry—for example, Sunday services, youth work, children's clubs, home groups, pastoral care and buildings maintenance. Each of these six areas of ministry could be thought of as a small pyramid in its own right, with an overall leader, assistants and so forth. If there are six leaders who work primarily in partnership with the minister, the church is operating CL. If, however, the six leaders work in equal partnership with the minister, their 'assistant leaders' and the church members, the church is operating CM. The question that begins to establish the style of leadership concerns the minister, because in both pyramidal leadership and CL he will be at the apex of the overall structure. So let's ask it: do these six areas of ministry collaborate with each other and church members, or do they contribute to a larger pyramid with the minister at the top? We can find out by asking two supplementary questions:

- Do the six areas of ministry look to the minister for direction?
- If there is a problem, does the minister sort it out?

If the answers are:

- 'Yes and yes', then however well delegated or collaborative the leadership is, the structure is pyramidal.
- 'Not always', then we are moving away from the traditional structure.
- 'No and no', then either our pyramid has broken down into anarchy (!) or we are working in the CM arena.

Pyramidal structures tend to establish centralization and encourage unhelpful dependency; collaboration tends to recognize diversity and encourage maturity. These issues are examined in later chapters, but for now let's just remember that delegated centralism and collaboration are not the same, and move on.

NEW TESTAMENT COLLABORATION

Jesus taught that his disciples would engage with God, each other and the world in a new way. In the early church, Christians attempted to do this as they developed a threefold structure of leadership. There were leaders with a wide geographical responsibility, others with tasks in a more narrow area, and others again in the role of assistants (1 Timothy 3:1–13; Titus 1:1–9). This threefold understanding was the basis for the historical pattern for church leadership (ordaining bishops, priests and deacons). In subsequent centuries, this original threefold ministry was elevated to the top of a new pyramidal structure, with all the attendant problems of power, wealth and corruption. The water was muddied when the biblical threefold ministry was used to justify the entire structure of the established church from the fourth century onwards, because it filled in the historical gaps with a later understanding. If we, in our own day, also do this with the biblical text, then we make the Bible say what it does not. The fact that there were *episcopos*, *presbyteros*, and *diakonos* is indisputable. What is under discussion is how these various leaders related to one another—and the ready presumption that they operated pyramidal leadership is not supported by the text.

In our own day, pyramidal structures can be responsible for the isolation and burn-out of church leaders while keeping congregations unhelpfully dependent and unfulfilled. Why? Because when pyramid leadership is operated in the church, human beings assume authority that belongs to God alone.

The New Testament leadership structure of the church looks something like this:

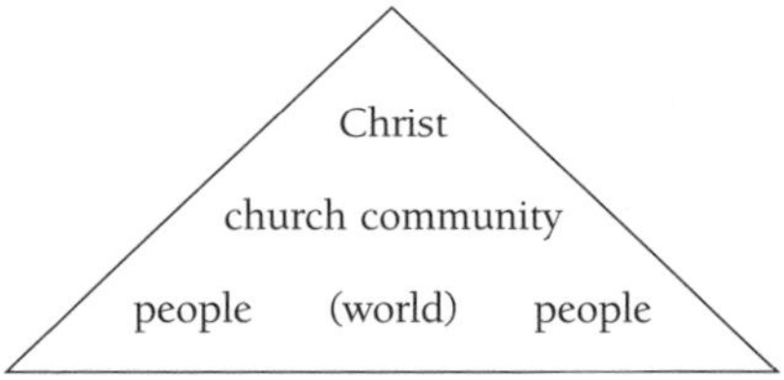

The structure is still a pyramid, akin to the Old Testament model noted in Chapter 1, but now, instead of the twin peaks of prophet and king, Jesus Christ fulfils both aspects of leadership and individual Christians relate directly to him. If the New Testament structure is drawn this way up, God is at the top and is able to 'direct' in an utterly self-giving way. It then becomes the 'Jesus model' viewed from the side. If the model is turned upside down (the servant leadership model), God, the foundation of our being, is big and strong enough to sustain the weight.

In this structure, the church community occupies the middle ground and is 'incarnate'—the gateway between the spirit and the flesh. The church, collaborating with the Holy Spirit, brings the concerns of the world to God and the concerns of God to the world. Whether in word or action, God works in the church to work through the church. Nothing that God gives to the church rests with the church; every gift of God is given away. Again, these attitudes will be carefully considered in the following chapters, but for now let's recognize that there is a problem with this leadership structure only when we emulate God and place ourselves at the apex of power and authority. This is original sin and goes right back to Eden, when human beings usurped the role of God and made decisions that belonged only to him. The Bible teaches that God never gave away either power or authority to human beings; he retains it.

CHRISTIAN COLLABORATION

The early Christians viewed leadership with Jesus at the top (or centre) and church leaders, assistant leaders and members of the congregation all occupying disciple positions around him. This means that the structure is only ever 'one person high', because every individual answers directly to the living God. If this understanding is related to a local church, we end up with something like this:

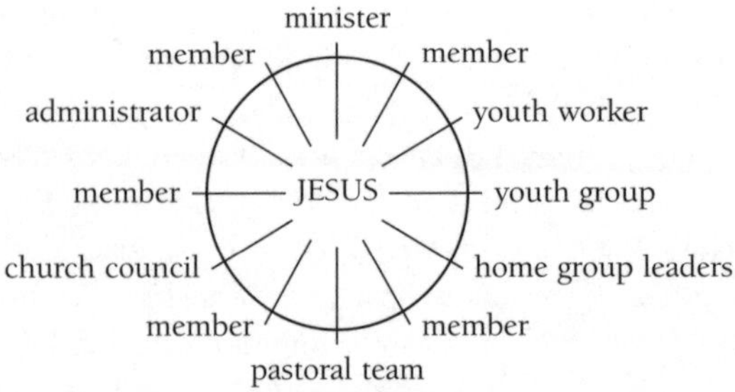

This diagram begins to outline, in practical terms, what CM is about. Drawing diagrams of any of the perimeter groups, such as the youth group, the pastoral team or the church council, would reveal an identical pattern of leadership (Jesus in the middle, with the ministry leader, other leaders and members gathered around him). Thus the whole church model is replicated in every part, and whether an individual, an area of ministry or the whole church is considered, the pattern is the same. Jesus always occupies the top spot because he is always at the centre with his disciples gathered around him.

Looking at the minister's role in the diagram, he is clearly near to some people and areas of ministry, and further away from others—which are next to a different selection of people and ministries. In a collaborative structure, different leaders share responsibilities across the church. The administrator in the diagram, for example, is closer to the church council than the minister is, and the home group leaders are closer to the pastoral team. This is just an example, not a blueprint for leadership, but what it begins to show is that the minister of this church will:

- Exercise appropriate leadership within some areas of church life.
- Work in other areas as an assistant leader (accepting the authority of those who are gifted in different areas of ministry).
- Receive ministry from others (after all, this is *his* church too; from where else will he receive spiritual care and sustenance?).
- Play no part at all in other areas.
- Submit to the leadership and authority of Jesus Christ, as a member of the whole church along with everyone else.

To those who are used to traditional pyramid leadership, the diagram above may look very much like a church that is out of control. This concern will be examined in Part Three, but for now, let's just acknowledge that this CM church isn't out of control. It's just that the way in which the minister (and other church leaders) relate to one another (and to church members) is very different from the formal, hierarchical pattern we may be used to.

A SUBTLE DIFFERENCE

Perhaps, at this stage, the difference between delegation and collaboration seems subtle to the point of being non-existent. Perhaps good delegation and collaboration appear to be identical, but they are not. The fundamental difference concerns where the buck stops, and although the choice is initially subtle, and because it is not a matter of leadership technique but of theological understanding, it shapes the life of the church. Our theology of authority is like a junction where we can proceed in one direction or another, and the divergence begins with our concept of Christian leadership.

If we think that leaders exist to get things done, then we shall move towards pyramidal delegation. In this model, the task of the minister is to move the congregation, as a unit, from one place to another place. How individuals feel about the move (or what they think about the minister) is only important in as much as negative feelings may hinder the work. Similarly, if we think that the task of minister is to increase the size of the congregation, then we shall proceed in this direction.

If we think that leaders exist to serve God, then we shall move towards CM, where the task is to ensure that members of the congregation grow and mature. The aim of every individual is to become, in some sense, a leader, because everyone occupies a 'ministerial space' between Christ and the world. In this model, the minister can only go as fast as the congregation and the eventual size of the congregation will be up to present members.

So, let's ask the question: what do we think Christian leadership is for? Are ministers there to get things done or to serve God, or both? We certainly presume that in a well-delegated pyramidal church, the members will grow and mature. The truth is that some will but the majority probably won't. We also fear that in a collaborative church, tasks won't get done. The truth is that the majority will, but some won't—and the things that don't get done might be the very things that are dearest to the pyramidal church.

In a typical pyramidal church, life will probably be efficiently organized, but the congregation will be dependent. In a collaborative church, more mistakes will probably be made, but the congregation will mature quickly (as will the minister!)

YES, BUT...

At this point we shall probably want to ask all sorts of questions. These questions may be negative:

- Surely, if the minister isn't in charge, the church will descend into anarchy? Won't the lack of a central leader encourage schism? How does a church like this get anything done? What if there are no leaders prepared to take on this kind of responsibility? Isn't the minister shirking his responsibilities? After all, he gets paid!

Or they may be positive:

- This makes a lot of sense, but how do you...? And what about when...?
- I think I've got a blurry image in my mind, but can you give me some clarity?
- Whatever you're selling, I'm buying... where do I sign?

Some of these queries and concerns will be answered in Part Three, when the impact of beginning a collaborative structure is considered and the pros and cons of this model of leadership are discussed. Meanwhile, fundamental queries and concerns will be addressed in Part Two, which defines CM by offering a biblical theology for ministry.

SOME QUESTIONS TO THINK ABOUT

1 In what ways is delegation easier than collaboration? In what ways is it more difficult?
2 When we collaborate, what do we gain, and what do we lose?
3 If a church changes from pyramidal leadership to CM, what is gained, and what is lost?

NOTE

1 'Sizing up a congregation for new ministry', Arlin Rothauge, 1983. This study is available free from: www.episcopalchurch.org/growth_4579_ENG_HTM.htm

Part Two

LAYING FOUNDATIONS

Chapter 5

SOME LESSONS FROM ACTS

In this part of the book, some biblical foundations are laid, so let's ask a foundational question: does God collaborate with human beings or are we his delegates on earth? The answer to this question has significant implications, and we may lean towards either of two extremes.

On the one hand, we might think in terms of 'God is in his heaven and we are here on earth'. If this is how we think about creation, we may feel that we are to steward the world as God's delegates—commissioned to do the best job possible and, at the end of our lives, judged on our performance. For us, worship may be a combination of remembrance (of the Christ who lived, died and ascended) and anticipation (of the better life ahead).

We may, on the other hand, lean towards the 'God is all in all' view. If this is how we think about creation, then we probably see our task as collaborating with God in all things as he continues to work in the world. For us, worship may be about sharing in the living presence of the divine as God moves among us here and now.

Looking at the book of Acts and the story of the church's birth, it's reasonable to ask, 'What did these Christians think they were doing? Did they think of themselves as delegates or collaborators?'

JESUS AND HIS DISCIPLES

The fact that Jesus had disciples highlights a fundamental truth: disciples follow their master (John 15:20). From time to time, volunteers appear in the Gospels, but some of these never get off the starting line (Matthew 8:21), for some the cost is too high (19:16–22) and for others their future lies elsewhere (Mark 5:18–20). There are also large numbers of people who follow Jesus, but when it comes to the crunch they drift away (John 6:66), except for the Twelve (vv. 67–69), and ultimately, of course, the Eleven (Acts 1:13), the women (v. 14) and those who were 'with them the whole time' (vv. 21–22).

The difference between a follower and a disciple is that the follower chooses his master but the master chooses his disciple. Jesus first calls the Twelve in the early chapters of each Gospel, but he confirms their relationship from time to time (John 6:70; 15:16), and it is close, constant and educative. For three years the disciples learn from Jesus and are changed by him. During this time he promises them that in the future, although he will leave them, they will receive the Holy Spirit who will continue the process (John 15:26—16:15). In fact, Jesus tells his disciples that it is better for them to be parted in order that the Spirit may come (John 16:7), and this becomes part of their message (Acts 2:38–39).

Turning from the Gospels to the book of Acts, we see that even though the disciples have been physically separated from Jesus by his death and then by his ascension, their relationship with him continues in two ways. Although he is no longer with them in a physical sense, they continue their bond with him through the presence of the Holy Spirit, continuing to call him Lord, seeking his direction and learning from him. Also, this relationship and knowledge are not for them alone but for everyone (Acts 2:39), and the post of disciple is now open to all. The church does not refer to its members as followers but as disciples (6:2), and each person receives the same spirit as the Twelve (2:38).

The book of Acts therefore shows an interesting development. Whereas, in the Gospels, ministry was delegated (Luke 10:1–20), it is now collaborative. When Jesus was 'with them' he sent them out by commissioning them. Now he 'goes with them' (Matthew 28:20) and shares the co-mission in the person of the Holy Spirit.

THE ACTS INITIATIVE

Acts 2 describes the coming of the Holy Spirit. He descends upon the gathering of believers and begins his work among them. The descent is actually quite noisy and noticeable, and a crowd gathers. Some people are impressed (v. 12) while others are not (v. 13), but the same question is asked by all: 'What does this mean?' It is a question that needs an answer, and as Peter stands up to provide one, a new partnership between God and his people can be seen. During the three years of Jesus' ministry, his words carried authority (Matthew 7:28–29) and now the words of Peter have the same kind of effect. He has not been changed by the death of Jesus or by the resurrection meetings: for the past 40 days he has been in hiding with the other disciples (John 20:19). Now, here he is preaching to thousands and his words prompt a spiritual response; he has been changed by the Holy Spirit and has entered into the partnership that Jesus promised.

The new partnership can be thought of like this: Peter speaks to the ears of his listeners and the Holy Spirit speaks to their hearts. As far as the crowd is concerned, Peter is the focus, but the truth is that Jesus is present and speaking to the men and women in the crowd. Just as it is the Holy Spirit who attracts the crowd through the tongues of the disciples, when Peter speaks, explains and makes connections with scripture it is the Spirit of Christ who speaks to the hearts of those listening.

Reading on (Acts 2:41), we see that many in the crowd respond. It should be noted that although 'many' of them believed (some 3000), this response wasn't universal and we don't know what proportion of the crowd made up the 3000. What we do know is that the new believers begin to behave like the other believers (vv. 42–47). These new Christians are disciples, not followers.

What we learn from the birth of the church is this:

- The Holy Spirit is active in both the 'minister' and the 'ministered to'.
- The Holy Spirit works in partnership with Peter, who speaks to the ear while the Spirit speaks to the heart.
- The telling includes both scripture and personal experience.

If Peter had said nothing, if he had chosen to keep silent, then the people in the crowd would have drawn their own conclusions and drifted away. Similarly, if the words had been Peter's alone, then maybe a few people would have been convinced and, while a few more stayed to argue, the majority would probably have lost interest. Also, until Peter spoke, no one in the crowd was eager to join the church. Even if the Holy Spirit was speaking to their hearts already, they could not recognize it until Peter opened his mouth.

This passage indicates in the most practical way that the promises of Jesus are beginning to be fulfilled. The people in the crowd have just been convicted of guilt, sin and judgment and convinced that Jesus is the Messiah, as Jesus said they would be (John 16:8–11). This is the work of the Holy Spirit (John 16:7) and, to accomplish it, God and Peter collaborate. The events of Pentecost were exceptional, but this fundamental pattern of ministry continued, which is why the apostles spoke of themselves as witnesses, and the Holy Spirit as witness, to the Lord Jesus Christ (Acts 5:32). Ministry had become a joint venture.

PHILIP AND THE ETHIOPIAN OFFICIAL

What is it like to collaborate with God? The pattern seems to be something like Matthew 14:22–31: ministry is akin to being asked to walk on water! If Jesus is not already standing there, disciples would be mad to try it; but even when they step out at his invitation, they don't always have sufficient faith and need rescuing. In Acts 8:26–40, Philip is obedient even when he has no clear idea about what he is being asked to do.

Let's look at this incident from three different points of view: through the eyes of Philip, through the eyes of the eunuch, and then from what might have been God's perspective.

Philip's story

What Philip was doing when an angel visited him is not stated in this passage. Perhaps he was at work, at prayer, or even taking out the rubbish. All the angel tells him is that he must go to the Gaza road (v. 26). He isn't told why, or where on the road to go—just to go, so that is what he does (v. 27). We don't know how long Philip was hanging about waiting, but at some point the Holy Spirit prompts him to go over to a chariot—which we would describe as an ox-drawn cart (v. 29). From this point, Philip receives no further promptings. As he jogs along beside the cart, he hears the man inside reading from Isaiah (silent reading is a modern concept). Taking the initiative, he asks the man if he understands the scripture (v. 30). At the man's invitation, Philip rides with him (v. 31), explains what he knows of Jesus the Messiah, and relates his experience to the scripture (v. 35). When the man requests it, Philip baptizes him (v. 38), and then 'the Spirit of the Lord takes him away' (vv. 39–40).

For Philip, this incident has various elements. There is the miraculous appearance of an angel and the clear prompting of the Holy Spirit. There is also a good deal of uncertainty (Where am I going? Why am I here? Who am I supposed to meet?). He also takes the initiative and responds to the man's requests.

The Ethiopian's story

The man was a royal official in the palace of the Ethiopian queen (v. 28)—hence the operation! No man was allowed to hold office close to the queen and remain 'intact', to ensure that there could be no gossip tainting either the honour of the monarch or the line of descent. This eunuch, though, was also a 'worshipper' of God, or a 'proselyte' (meaning that he had embraced the Hebrew faith), who had been to worship in Jerusalem. He could not convert fully (even if he wanted to) because his operation precluded him (Deuteronomy 23:1). Because he was visiting Jerusalem, it is unlikely that he had not heard about the new Christian church and the persecution (Acts 8:1–3). Perhaps he had also heard something about the death of Stephen, the Pentecost of Acts 2 and the Passover festival when Jesus was crucified.

He is now returning home, and as he travels he is reading Isaiah (vv. 32–33). The Gaza road is a major route for traffic and the Ethiopian is travelling with his own entourage, but in the general throng he becomes aware of a man at his elbow asking him if he understands what he is reading (v. 30). Gratefully, he invites the man to join him (v. 31) and explain it (v. 34). The man connects the scriptures to Jesus, and it all makes sense to the Ethiopian. He asks if he might be baptized (v. 36), which is a big question. He is a eunuch, not fully accepted into his chosen religion, so will he be accepted by these people? He is baptized (v. 38), and then left to continue his journey—which he does, rejoicing (v. 39).

We trust that this Ethiopian also received the Holy Spirit and that his rejoicing was a spiritual as well as a natural reaction to God's acceptance of him. Who this man was, we do not know, but at about this time there was a missionary bishop in Ethiopia who was a eunuch, so perhaps…?

The Lord's perspective

This is, of course, pure speculation, but perhaps we can imagine a third perspective. The Holy Spirit has been at work in the Ethiopian for years. He has brought him from a pagan religion into Hebrew faith and sustained him through some considerable personal difficulties. On this visit to Jerusalem, the Spirit has been speaking to the man. Ironically, in a city stuffed with Christians, he was not ready to hear, but on the way home, he is. There are thousands of believers in Jerusalem who could have spoken to this man, but there is no one on the road he travels. So the Lord sends a message to Philip: he must get himself down on the road straight away. When Philip arrives, the Holy Spirit shows him the carriage and tells him to go alongside (just as the Spirit is highlighting Isaiah 53 for the Ethiopian).

During the conversation between the two men, as Philip speaks to the Ethiopian's ears the Spirit speaks to his heart. When the Ethiopian's heart turns, the Lord forgives him, and when he is prompted into baptism, the Spirit fills him. There is a party in heaven (Luke 15:10) and God blesses his Ethiopian child by sharing the joy with him.

Although this third story is complete speculation, in reality there are always three stories. Christian ministry is never a purely human activity; it is always a collaboration between the Holy Spirit and human beings. Why did God bother going through the rigmarole of getting Philip to the Gaza road? Why didn't God just speak to the Ethiopian directly? Because God chooses to work collaboratively with the church; God chooses to speak to the heart when a disciple speaks to the ear. If there is no Philip, there is no Ethiopian convert. Similarly, Philip does as he is told. Presumably Philip didn't spend his leisure time lurking about on the Gaza road on the off-chance of meeting someone interested in Isaiah! He wasn't a volunteer, speculating down every avenue of potential ministry; he was a disciple, doing as he was told.

REACHING THE ENDS OF THE EARTH

In the early chapters of Acts, the good news about Jesus spreads like ripples from the centre of a pool. Initially, the church witnessed in Jerusalem, Judea and Samaria. The word was proclaimed in ripples, outwards, and the next ripple was the big one, because it included the 'ends of the earth'. And who does God choose to take this leap? Someone with a proven record for being good at risk-taking, the water-walker himself—Peter.

Two visions

In Acts 10:1–16, God continues to minister collaboratively and gives two visions. The first is given to Cornelius, a Gentile who was both devout and 'God-fearing': an angel visits and tells him to send for Peter (vv. 4–6). He is not told why he should do this, but he is given instructions that locate Peter, so Cornelius does what he is told: he sends servants to fetch him (vv. 7–8). As the servants make their way to Joppa, Peter is given the second vision (vv. 9–16). He sees a large sheet with all kinds of animals in it. The Lord tells him to kill and eat, declaring that nothing is unclean. For Peter, used to dietary restrictions and ritual purity, this is such a leap in his thinking that he has difficulty accepting it. He has to be given the same vision three times.

As Peter's vision ends, Cornelius' servants arrive (vv. 17–18). Peter is still trying to puzzle out the meaning of what he has seen when the Holy Spirit tells him that three men have come looking for him and that he is to go with them (he is not told why) (vv. 19–20). Peter greets them and introduces himself as the one they are seeking (v. 21). They tell him that 'a holy angel told [Cornelius] to have you come to his house so that he could hear what you have to say' (v. 22). This is quite an invitation—after all, what *has* Peter got to say to them? So Peter promptly… procrastinates, and invites them to stay the night (v. 23a).

The next day, he takes some other church members and travels with Cornelius' servants to Caesarea (v. 23b). When they arrive at Cornelius' house, they find that he has gathered his friends and relatives (v. 24). Peter explains that he has had a vision which allows him now to visit Gentile people. They discover that their visions are connected and Cornelius assures Peter that they are expectantly waiting to hear what God has told him to say (vv. 25–33).

Peter then just talks about Jesus and proclaims that those who believe in Jesus will be forgiven their sins (vv. 34–43). While he is still talking, the Holy Spirit falls upon the assembled Gentiles, and when Peter sees what has happened he orders that they be baptized (vv. 44–48).

There are some key things to learn from this incident:

- Neither Peter nor anyone else in the church was expecting God to bring salvation to the Gentiles in this way. These Christians were not looking in the Gentiles' direction, but because they were looking at Jesus, they were disciples ready to take the master's lead.
- The Lord gave visions that brought the two parties together, but neither side was given every detail. Only by putting the two visions together could any sense be made of each.
- When Peter eventually spoke, were his words actually that important? After all, he wasn't told what to say, and the Holy Spirit didn't even wait for him to finish. In this case, obedience seems to have been more important than the content of Peter's talk. This whole event was a learning curve for Peter: agreeing to visit a Gentile home was a big step for him (v. 28).
- In the end, the Lord just dealt directly with the Gentiles, so why involve Peter at all? Because although the Holy Spirit speaks to the heart, he works with his disciple Peter, who speaks to the ear. Also, the Spirit was teaching Peter something: in this sense, Peter and Cornelius were on level ground as they each learned from Christ. Jesus was showing Peter in absolute terms that the

promise Peter himself had spoken of on the day of Pentecost, 'for you and your children and for all who are far off—for all whom the Lord our God will call' (Acts 2:39), applied to these Gentile people too. Through Peter, the Holy Spirit was teaching this truth to the church. It is noticeable that later on, when Paul was called to account for his activities among the Gentiles, it was Peter who most clearly understood what God was doing (Acts 15:1–21).

- It's worth noting that when Peter got home he was criticized (Acts 11:1–4). Perhaps a reflective pause would be appropriate here!

COLLABORATING WITH GOD

Why should Christians collaborate together in ministry? Because God collaborates with us. Wherever we look in the New Testament, the same pattern is seen. The Holy Spirit collaborates with those who minister and also with those receiving that ministry. He is at work in the hearts of both and can be rejected by either. Not every minister is obedient, and not every 'receiver of ministry' receives it. Yet it is always a threefold process. Without the Holy Spirit, preaching is likely to be interesting (or boring) words of hope; with the Holy Spirit, it becomes the word of life. Without the Holy Spirit, action is likely to be well-intentioned (or misguided) effort; with the Holy Spirit, it becomes life-changing.

What we see in Acts and in the rest of the New Testament is a model of ministry in which disciples look directly to the risen Christ as their master. Sometimes, when called to minister, they find that they learn something new and vital themselves. They recognize that God often has his own timetable and that they are required to step out in faith, without knowing every detail of his plan. In this we see the heart of their collaborative attitude: they expect God to engage actively with them in ministry, otherwise they are left dangling. These are not 'experts', doling out their expertise; these are disciples, discovering as they go what God is doing. In this, they mirror the attitude of their master (John 12:49).

As far as we are concerned:

- If we think in terms of 'my ministry', then delegation and pyramidal leadership will probably seem natural to us.
- If we think of ministry as 'Jesus' ministry, in which I assist', then CM will be on our agenda.
- If we understand ministry to be something that the Holy Spirit shares with us, then sharing it with one another in CM becomes second nature.

Chapter 6

A HOLY PRIESTHOOD

In the past, CM was called 'shared ministry', but the two are not the same. 'Shared ministry' tends to mean 'the minister sharing his tasks (but not his role) with others'. A whole range of people may be involved in 'doing things', but they will be under the minister's direction, and if they do not meet his standards he will probably give the task to someone else. In CM, the whole church shares the ministerial role because tasks are a consequence of gifting. Shared ministry is like a dinner party where the host trusts certain individuals to prepare and serve the food on his behalf; CM is more like a 'bring and share' supper. The two approaches differ because they each rest on a different understanding of authority.

THE DOMINO EFFECT

How a church is organized depends, in large part, on how Christ's authority is viewed. We talked in the Introduction about the three key aspects of any leadership structure: authority, acceptance and covenant. If we imagine a line of dominoes standing upright, waiting for the first domino to be pushed, then 'authority' is the last domino before a junction where two lines of dominoes go off in different directions. If the 'authority' domino topples to the left, it pushes into 'acceptance' and then 'covenant' in a particular way. Basically, if authority is vested in the minister, he may retain, or wish to share, ministry with church members. If the 'authority' domino topples to the right, however, then it pushes 'acceptance' and 'covenant' towards a different conclusion. This time, because authority remains with Christ, he is the one who shares ministry with both the minister and the members. The understanding of authority, acceptance and covenant therefore determines the approach to leadership, membership and the relationship between the two. If the dominos tip one way, we pursue pyramidal structures; if they tip the other way, we pursue CM. Our understanding of authority is where the divergence begins.

This chapter considers authority by looking at the development of priesthood through the Old Testament and comparing it with New Testament expectations. To say that a theology of priesthood is biblical is one thing; to recognize where in the Bible it is located is another. If, for example, a theology of priesthood is largely Old Testament in origin, then the subsequent understanding of leadership will be shaped by that origin, as will the understanding of membership and the relationship between leaders and members.

A concept of priesthood is central to any understanding of biblical authority. On this subject, in terms of doctrine, different denominations and non-denominational churches are poles apart, yet in terms of practice, many are indistinguishable. The minister in the example above, who shares ministry, is actually behaving in a priestly fashion, so a church leader may be called a 'minister' or some other title but when his role within the church is scrutinized, his actions and authority may mirror those of a 'priest'. It is therefore unhelpful to focus on titles; it is much more fruitful to consider our understanding of what 'ministers' are doing when they engage in their leadership role, and what we think they are doing will depend, in large part, on our theology of authority.

PRIESTHOOD AND RELIGION

The concept of priesthood only makes sense in a world where human beings are in some way separated from the divine, because the priest then acts as an intermediary or go-between. He is the person who 'gatekeeps' between the divine and the people, because he is acceptable to both. The relationship can be pictured as an hourglass, in which the god occupies the upper circle, the people occupy the lower circle and the priest occupies the constricted space between the two. The priest's intermediary role involves bringing the concerns of the god to the people, and the concerns of the people to the god. Most cultures have people who perform this role and, although their titles might be different (they might be called a witch doctor, a guru, a priest or a hundred other names), their task is the same. They stand in the 'gate' between the spiritual and the physical, between heaven and earth, between the gods and human beings. In some religions, the emphasis is bottom up, and the focus is on bringing the concerns of the faithful to the attention of their god. In other religions, the emphasis is top down and focuses on bringing the concerns of the gods to the faithful. As a general rule, the second type of religion tends to be more dictatorial, with priests wielding greater personal power.

It is also true, human nature being what it is, that even within different religions there will be certain individuals who disagree about where the emphasis is placed. In Christian history, there are both ministers and members who emphazise 'our humble approach to God', while others in the same church emphazise 'our need to obey his commands'. It's an interesting question to ask of our own church: do we balance bringing human concerns to God with bringing his concerns to us, or do we tend to tip towards one emphasis or the other? Do we see the priest (and here 'priest' is shorthand for 'main church leader', whatever his title in our church) as primarily assisting the people or receiving orders from God?

If human beings are separated from God, then an intermediary is needed to stand in the gap.

SIN AND SEPARATION

Genesis 1—3 speaks about the creation of the world and the fall of human beings. God creates human beings in a way that makes it possible for them to know their Creator, but human sin spoils this relationship with God, with one other, and with the world they inhabit (3:16–19). Although life is different after the fall, God still makes himself known (Genesis 4:6; 6:13), and he does not simply destroy everything and start again (9:11). Thus we are left with a conundrum: God is knowable and wishes to be known, but human sin removes human beings from the presence of God. There is a gap with no intermediary.

From the beginning, God chooses to act 'incarnately' in the world; that is to say, it is human beings who steward the physical world (Genesis 1:28). Their stewardship, however, has a spiritual content which is defined by their relationship with God. Thus human beings are the first 'incarnate intermediaries' or 'priesthood' through whom God interfaces with his creation.[1] Because of human sin, this first 'incarnate priesthood' collapses; there is separation (3:22–24) and a new priesthood is needed.

In Genesis 12:1–6, God called Abram to leave his homeland and become the founder of a new nation. This would be achieved through paternity and, although Abram and Sarai struggled with infertility (Genesis 16), Isaac was the fulfilment of God's promise (18:1–15; 21:1–8). When Isaac married Rebecca (24:67), the nation expanded through him, and then, through Jacob's sons, into the tribes of Israel. Thus, God's incarnate way of relating to his creation continues, although now he relates through a family.

As was mentioned in Chapter 1, Abraham, Isaac and Jacob combined the roles of prophet, priest and king. They not only led; they also fulfilled a religious role—erecting stones (Genesis 28:22) and altars (35:3), making sacrifices (22:1–13) and circumcising (17:23). They are described as being on familiar terms with God and he revealed to them different facets of his nature. God is referred to as the 'Shield of Abraham' (Genesis 15:1), the 'Fear of Isaac' (31:42) and the 'Mighty One of Jacob' (49:24) and the three patriarchs personally became 'priests', standing between God and his people.

Although Moses was the same kind of leader, it is in the book of Exodus that formal religion is instituted. Exodus 19:10–11 describes purification for worship and 29:1–37 describes the priesthood. There are detailed descriptions of priestly garb and activity (ch. 28; 29:38—30:38), the founding of the sabbath (31:12–17) and the establishment of a tent of meeting (31:1–11), and instructions about sacred objects (chs. 25 and 27). In these passages, the 'tent of meeting' is set up as a precursor to the temple in Jerusalem first built by Solomon (1 Kings 6).

The priesthood is described in Exodus, but it didn't really operate at this time. For example, although the tent of meeting was open to all, it was Moses who mediated between God and the people, not priests (33:7–11). Even with the tent of meeting and the priesthood, the 'gap' between God and his people was very wide and God's holiness precluded all except Moses from entering his presence. Therefore, even when the meeting place was a mountain, the people could not come near (19:12–13).

There is a promise, however. Although the temple and its priesthood were founded, and although in reality it was Moses who functioned as priest to the nation, the whole nation had a priestly character (19:5–6) towards other nations. They were not only a 'chosen people' in the sense that they had a special relationship with God; they were also to be a kingdom of priests and a holy nation for the world. We are left now to speculate on the meaning of this.

THE DEVELOPMENT OF THE PRIESTHOOD

From the first temple built by Solomon, through the second temple built after the exiles returned with Nehemiah, to the third temple built by Herod the Great (still unfinished in Jesus' lifetime), there was a 'tent of meeting' located within the building that contained the sacred objects mentioned in Exodus 25 and 27. It consisted of the Holy Place and also the Most Holy Place (Exodus 26:33–34), or 'Holy of Holies'. The curtain that separated the Holy Place from the Most Holy Place was part of the link to the original tent. In Herod's grand temple, it was some 18 x 9 metres, and ten centimetres thick. The Most Holy Place was regarded as the dwelling place of God, and the high priest alone could enter, once a year, on the Day of Atonement. Thus God dwelt among his people, yet they were separated from him, and priests were the intermediaries.

In each generation, worship was maintained by the priesthood, which was defined by birth, not calling. Although this religious leadership was very complex (and there was also politicking and change over the centuries), broadly speaking, priests and high priests were descendants of Levi's son Kohath (Aaron was of this lineage), and Levites were descendants of Levi's other sons, Gershon and Merari. The distinction between priests and Levites was sometimes blurred, but by New Testament times the priests presided over ritual while the Levites were concerned with teaching the law. In addition, there were the various 'denominations' (such as Pharisees and Sadducees), scribes and lawyers. To get some idea of the scale of this religious leadership, it helps to read Ezra 2:36–39 and 1 Chronicles 23:3. There were so many priests that they needed to be organized into 'classes' (1 Chronicles 23:4–5; 24:7–18). Priestly duties were organized by rota (Luke 1:8) and there was a multitude of priestly families.

The high priest (Leviticus 21:10–15) presided over the Sanhedrin (the national religious court) and over a group of chief priests (Acts 25:2). He too was only one high priest among many, so again there was a rota (John 18:13). The Levites assisted the high priest and the chief priests by being responsible for temple maintenance, teaching, providing music and so forth. Priests and Levites were busy men because there were sacrifices every day and a complex calendar of religious feasts. Even so, there were too many, and it is on record that many of them lived out their lives (supported by tithes and working in business) without ever being called for temple duty.

SACRIFICE

To understand priesthood and the temple, it helps to understand sacrifice. There were different categories of sacrifice, some of which were more costly than others (Leviticus 1—7). The same rule applied to all, though: the sacrifice must be of the highest quality and without defect. The principle was this: human beings inhabit God's creation (it is not ours but his), so humility is shown and his Lordship is recognized when that which is most expensive is sacrificed. Sacrifice recognizes that everything that human beings have and are belongs to God, and in the destruction of an offering there is an acknowledgment that we are in the wrong, that God is in the right, and a restoration of relationship is sought.

In the early days of the Hebrew people, anyone could make their own sacrifice (Exodus 12:21). As they settled as a nation, however, a professional priesthood evolved (Judges 17:5–13) and, with the building of the first temple, it had a location. This formalized both the priestly role and the structure of leadership. From this position, priests and Levites became the educated class of Israel, and without them we would have no Old Testament to read. By New Testament times, wealthy aristocratic families occupied the pinnacle of the national pyramid and spiritually they were in charge of a system that gatekept the gap between God and his people. By this time, religion was definitely a top-down structure, with priests and Levites emphasizing the need for obedience (Luke 11:46, 52). The temple was the place of meeting; only there might sin be addressed (Leviticus 1:1–9), and only priests could do this through sacrificial mediation.

JESUS AND THE PRIESTHOOD

During the three years of his ministry, Jesus' own lack of priestly, levitical or rabbinic qualifications did not go unnoticed by either the people (Matthew 13:53–57) or the priesthood (21:23). His criticism of religious leaders (16:6; 23:1–39) enraged them and they plotted his downfall (26:3–4). He was arrested, brought to trial and crucified (27:41–43).

To the priests, Jesus was no different from a dozen other insurgents who had set themselves up in defiance of their authority. What only a few priests understood (John 3:1–21; 19:39) was that, in Jesus, all things would be made new (2 Corinthians 5:17). Jesus himself was the 'gateway' between God and his people (John 10:7) and the cross of Christ became the entrance into God's holy presence (Colossians 1:20). The priests planned to remove Jesus (and his challenge to their authority) by bringing him to crucifixion, and in the process they lost the system that they sought to retain (Ephesians 2:14–16). When the curtain in the temple was ripped apart (Mark 15:38), the Holy of Holies, the tent of meeting, became open to all. With open access to this inner dwelling place of God, the intermediary priesthood of the old covenant was over.

During the 40 days between his resurrection and ascension, Jesus explained to his disciples the connection between their present experience and their scriptural understanding (Luke 24:25–27, 44–46). He also prepared them for what was ahead (v. 49). On the day of Pentecost, the Holy Spirit filled the believers (Acts 2:1–4) and, in very short order, new believers too (v. 38), of whom many were old covenant priests (6:7). God was now with his people and they were in his presence, and the incarnate gateway and curtain was Jesus Christ. He, in his own person, 'is the way' to the Father (John 14:6) and the way is open, not closed.

The new Adam has succeeded where the first Adam fell (1 Corinthians 15:20–22, 42–49). The creation is restored and the relationship between God and his creation re-established. God, who wishes to be known, may now be known through Christ, and the role of the priest is subsumed into him. There is now one incarnate intermediary between God and human beings (John 11:25–26): Jesus. Thus the old covenant is not abolished but fulfilled (Matthew 5:17–20).

JESUS, THE GREAT HIGH PRIEST

In accordance with the sacrificial system, Jesus becomes the sacrifice (Romans 5:6–11) and, in so doing, replaces its temporary nature with a permanent sacrifice for sin (Hebrews 10:3–4, 10). Thus the old requirement for sacrifice is both satisfied and super-seded by the one, sufficient sacrifice of Christ.

In the new covenant, the sacrifice is also the high priest (Hebrews 8:1–2). He has, as it were, presided over the defining sacrifice of history (Hebrews 9:14); he intercedes on behalf of sinners (7:25), speaks to human beings (12:25) and occupies the real (spiritual or heavenly) temple, of which the earthly temple was only a copy. There is now, therefore, no temple and no priesthood according to the Old Testament pattern, because there is no more need for sacrifice. Jesus has fulfilled his promise that in his own body he would tear down and rebuild the temple (John 2:19). He now dwells in the Holy of Holies (Hebrews 9:24), and Christians, because of his death, may join him (10:21–22).

THE PRIESTHOOD OF CHRISTIANS

According to the letter to the Hebrews, in the new covenant there is a new priesthood (see, for example, chapters 8 and 9). It follows the same pattern as the old priesthood, but it is now defined by the Spirit. The new priests are still related to the high priest, Christ, in that they are called 'brothers' (Hebrews 2:11). Jesus has become the 'new Aaron' and, because believers are 'born again of water and the Spirit' (John 3:3, 5), those made holy through Christ join the 'priestly family'. Duties involve offering praise and sacrifice after the pattern of Jesus—crosses taken up (Matthew 16:24) and lives laid down (Romans 12:1). This significant shift from old covenant priesthood to a priesthood of all believers can be thought of as the second aspect of the tearing of the temple curtain. As well as human beings 'going in' through the curtain, God the Holy Spirit 'comes out'.

It is against this background that Christians are described as priests. 1 Peter 2:5 speaks of a 'holy priesthood' and this is further defined by verse 9, which adds 'royal', 'chosen people' and 'holy nation'. All Christian people, whether they are ministers or members, are called to mediate (for example, by prayerfully bringing the concerns of people to God and by speaking of a personal faith, which brings the concerns of God to people), so every Christian is an intermediary who shares the priestly task. Paul uses this phraseology when he speaks of his ministry to the Gentiles (Romans 15:16), yet his leadership title is 'apostle', not 'priest'. In other words, in New Testament thinking, the title of priest is connected with task, not role. Thus, every previous priestly position (role) is attached to Christ, while the church is expected to share the priestly task. This new covenant priesthood describes not only 'new temple worship' but a fulfilment of Exodus 19:5–6: Christians are the priestly nation. This same image is used in Revelation 1:6, 20:6 and, connected with Exodus 19, in Revelation 5:10.

To sum up, the human race is finally back where it started in Genesis 2. Under the old covenant, the priesthood kept the gate between God and his people, and the 'holy nation' kept the gate between God and his world. Under the new covenant, Christ himself is the gate between God and all people, while the 'Christian nation' offers this open gate to the world.

PRIESTHOOD IN THE CHURCH

Moving into the Dark Ages (AD400 onwards), Old Testament theology seems to re-emerge in the church. To over-exaggerate, the old covenant copy was replaced by new covenant reality, but then the church re-established the copy. It was different from the old covenant in that the single temple in Jerusalem was replaced by a 'mini temple' in each locality—but the theology was the same. The church building was seen as a holy space, and the sanctuary, which contained an altar, was regarded as particularly holy. Here, the sacrifice of Christ was located in bread and wine, and there were sacred objects and rituals. In this new Holy of Holies, only priests could mediate, and at the height of this tradition the 'Holy Place' was screened off and made accessible only to priests, who alone received the bread and wine. Everyone else attended by being present in the body of the church building.

This new priesthood was identical, in its structure of leadership, to Old Testament priesthood. It was strictly pyramidal with only one man at the top, and in this 'Christian' version there was no rota. This Christian priesthood, with its complex structure of authority, related to the people in a top-down fashion. Spiritually, priests resumed the old covenant role of gatekeepers between God and his people.

It was against this theology and practice that the Puritans and Protestants of the 17th century rebelled. When, for example, they hacked down altars and replaced them with tables, they were making an unequivocal theological statement about the nature of Christ's sacrifice. Some Christian denominations still retain the medieval pattern of priesthood; other denominations don't. The Church of England, for example, continues to ordain according to 'apostolic succession'. That is to say, only those who have been ordained by those who have been ordained (by those who, in their turn, have been ordained... and so on, right back up the chain to the time when the apostles laid their hands on others for ministry) are recognized as being ordained.

Similarly, Anglicans ordain to the threefold ministry of bishops, priests and deacons. There is no room here to consider the arguments connected with this threefold ordination, but they are covered in depth in other books on leadership. Here, we simply recognize that it is a tenable and reasonable interpretation of the New Testament, and focus on the practical application. Broadly speaking, all three orders of ministry vow to serve God, the church and humankind, but deacons promise to assist ministry, priests promise to minister in a locality, and bishops promise to oversee this ministry across a geographical area. There is an affirmation that each ordination adds to the previous ordination rather than replacing it. Therefore, a priest retains his office of deacon, and a bishop is also a deacon and a priest. Within the Church of England, there are different interpretations of what these offices mean. Some hold a presbyterian view (that ordination is a setting apart for ministry), while others hold a catholic view (that each ordination ontologically changes the person being ordained). Thus, some people see ordination in terms of task while others see it in terms of being.

To Christians from other denominations, this may seem irrelevant, but it isn't. Each church establishes and evolves a pattern of leadership. It may or may not carry the title of 'priesthood' and it may trace its roots into history or into contemporary culture, but whatever our ancient or modern past, the same issues face us all. To organize our church, we shall need assistant leaders, main leaders and overseers—the same pattern that we see in the New Testament church. Most Christians will probably want to point to the biblical offices and relate them to their own leadership structure. The central issue, though, is not what these leaders are called, whether they are ordained, commissioned or appointed, or even where the structure came from. The central issue concerns how these leaders relate to God and to those whom they lead.

In a nutshell, in the Old Testament, priesthood was located in the individual. In the New Testament it was located in Christ, and at Pentecost it was exercised through the church. The community nature of Christian priesthood will be considered in later chapters. For now, there is a key question to ask: where, in our church, do we locate priesthood? In individuals, in Christ, in the church body—where?

WHERE DO WE LOCATE PRIESTHOOD?

If priesthood is located in old covenant theology, then a church will be dependent on specific leaders. The structure will be pyramidal and it will operate top-down leadership. The pyramidal nature of this leadership may be shared or may be considered as some form of servant leadership, but it will be delegated by the pinnacle person. In this Old Testament style of leadership, the pinnacle leader will not only gatekeep between God and the people; he will also gatekeep leadership, and assistant leaders will be chosen and affirmed by him.

If priesthood is located in New Testament theology, it will probably still end up as an Old Testament model. This happens because Christ is rightly placed at the top, but a clerical hierarchy is put between him and the people. In practical action, this kind of church will look no different from those churches that locate their theology of priesthood in the old covenant. Why? Because operating this kind of leadership relies on the ascended Christ ruling from the throne of heaven… and staying there! As he is not here on earth, the Christian priesthood ministers in his stead and, effectively, gatekeeps on his behalf until his return. This kind of leadership will probably also display shared or delegated leadership, stemming from and answerable to the pinnacle leader.

If priesthood is located in a theology of Pentecost, then it will be closer to that of the early church. Recognizing that Jesus is the one high priest and that Christians, through the power and presence of the Holy Spirit, share the priestly task reflects early church thinking about Christ, the church and the human race. Because priesthood is concerned with sharing tasks rather than assuming roles, there is no misunderstanding about who is in charge. When Christ is in authority, collaboration between ministers and members, rather than delegation, becomes an appropriate model of leadership.

The practical application of this theology will be explored further in Part 3. For now, the focus is priesthood and the recognition that whenever the church shares the priestly task, it behaves as a 'priesthood of all believers'. The fact that the church needs leaders (and that some churches ordain these people while other churches commission or appoint them) is not relevant to this new covenant priestly task. Leadership, whether we call it priesthood, ministry or anything else, is a specific task within the church. Priesthood, in the New Testament sense, is the corporate task of the whole church and relevant to both 'going out' and 'building up'. It is the task, in collaboration with the Spirit, of sharing with others what we know of the one high priest and sacrifice, Jesus, and pointing to him as the open curtain into the holy presence of God.

When the priestly role (rather than task) that belongs to Christ alone is relocated in human beings, then the opening created when the temple curtain tore from top to bottom becomes blocked up once more. The place of dwelling that was made open by Christ, and the role of intermediary which is his alone, are closed off again as human beings stand in the gateway between heaven and earth. As a consequence, the Old Testament pattern of (pyramidal) leadership is retained. Unless our understanding of priesthood is not only New Testament but post-Pentecostal, our chances of embracing CM are slim.

NOTES

1 There is a fuller exploration of this theme in Chapter 1 of *Marriage—Restoring Our Vision* (David Robertson, BRF, 2005).

Chapter 7

THE HOUSEHOLD OF FAITH

For many years Christians have embraced 'the family' as an appropriate model of being church. Many congregations provide a 'Family Service' at least once a month and social gatherings often contain the word 'family' in the advertising blurb. Although this term has now largely been replaced with the 'all-age' tag, we still hear Christians referring to 'the church family'.

The image is popular because it's Bible-based, but using 'Bible-based' imagery is not necessarily the same thing as being 'true to the Bible'. In the recent past, the concept of family has tended to aspire towards cosy security, in contrast to the biblical understanding in which the father's word was at the heart of the family and was, quite literally, law. Similarly, the concept often takes no account of the connected image of 'household'. In the present day, we find ourselves not only one step away from the biblical concepts of family and household, but also far removed from the traditional British understanding of family (father, mother and 2.4 children). As a general comment, in a culture where 'family' has a plethora of meanings, it may be helpful for Christians to rediscover the biblical meaning of 'household', but when it comes to a concept of authority, the biblical understanding of 'head of the household' has a significant impact. When it is accepted that it is Jesus who is the head, the attitude to leadership becomes different (as Jesus said it would).

Let's look at the Bible passages upon which these images are based.

THE FAMILY OF FAITH

One of the passages foundational to 'family' is Ephesians 3:14–15, in which Paul says that our heavenly Father gives all families their name. To understand his teaching, it is helpful to recognize Paul's background (Philippians 3:5). Genesis 1:26–27 says that God created the human race (male and female) in his own image. Over the centuries, Hebrew scholars developed several doctrines from this passage, and the one pertinent to this study was their view of family. By the time Paul was being educated, these verses in Genesis had developed into an understanding that, to put it crudely, if you wanted to have some idea of what God was like, you had to look at a married couple or perhaps at God's chosen people (the Hebrew nation), because God was simply too 'big' to see his image in any individual person. Here in Ephesians, Paul is probably thinking along this track, because in verse 9 he describes God as the creator of all things before moving on to focus on God's fatherhood and the family of humankind. He says that the way back into the Father's presence is now opened by Christ (the gate, the torn curtain, the high priest), and all may 'approach... with freedom and confidence' (v. 12); God's image is restored (v. 19) and there is one family because there is one Father.

Another representative passage is 1 John 2:9–11, where Christians are described as 'brothers'. Similarly, James 2:15–17 mentions 'brothers and sisters' and 1 Timothy 5:1–2 refers to the whole family. By using this kind of terminology, these writers are echoing the words of Jesus (Luke 8:19–21). So there is ample New Testament material that allows us to think of the church as a family. The question is, what kind of family? Does our own traditional concept of 'home and family' shape our view of 'church family'? In other words, do our cultural expectations colour our interpretation of the Bible?

In a way, this is a trick question, because if Paul is right in Ephesians 3:14–15 and every family takes its name from the father, then each must influence the other. This will mean that in any culture there will be some wonderful reflections of God's fatherhood as well as some depressingly awful failures. This will hold true for both the first century and our own day; but that is not the point. Unless we appreciate what first-century Christians thought 'family' looked like, we shall misunderstand the point they were making when they applied this image to the church.

FIRST-CENTURY CHRISTIANS

For first-century Christians, history had been newly redefined by Christ's redemption. The first Adam (responsible for the fall) had been superseded by the second Adam, Jesus Christ (1 Corinthians 15:45). This second Adam did not fall, but took upon himself the consequences of the fall. He became the second founder of the human race, of a new family with the same heavenly Father. This new race could, through faith, also trace its ancestry to Abraham (Romans 4:11). It had been 'grafted in' to the original root (Romans 11:17) and the task was the same: the new race, or new nation (or new family), was to bring redemption to the world.

The practical outworking of this worldview can be seen in Acts 2:43–47, where we read that the Christians in Jerusalem shared their lives and possessions. To appreciate what was happening there, it needs to be understood that this kind of behaviour was usual only within the family. In a society where there was no welfare state and little in the way of formally distributed charity, it was up to the family to tend to the practical needs of its own members. What makes Acts 2 remarkable is that people who were not related to each other behaved as if they were. The church regarded itself as a family and expressed this view through close fellowship, attitudes to property, meeting together in a large group (like an extended family) and in small groups (like intimate family units) in humility and prayer. They were living in a relationship with each other that had nothing to do with blood ties but was the living embodiment of Jesus' prophetic declaration in Matthew 10:34–39. They recognized God as their mutual Father and behaved accordingly, under his authority.

So here is the real question: when we, in our culture, use the words 'church family', 'family service' or 'family picnic', is this concept remotely like that of the first-century church? Truthfully, the answer is probably 'No'. The first-century Christian family mirrored family as they knew it, which was extended and inclusive. Our own patterns of family life have tended to be nuclear and exclusive. In the first century, the image helped people to turn outwards and welcome strangers as if they were family. In the modern era, it has often encouraged people to think of joining the church as becoming members of an exclusive club.

If any church today chooses to pattern itself after first-century family life rather than the traditional British family structure, it makes a clear counter-cultural statement and will attract attention. In our individualistic society, people are hungry for community.

THE HOUSEHOLD OF FAITH

Whatever our background, there is one constant factor in family life, and that is the blindingly obvious fact that family members are related to each other! This might seem too inane to mention, but it is important to note that personal choice has no bearing on the matter. As we say in our culture, 'You can choose your friends, but not your family.' When it comes to family, we are either blessed with them or stuck with them—and they with us. A first-century household was another matter, however. It contained not only the family (immediate and extended, with cousins, aunts and so on), but also servants, slaves and their families too. This was a culture in which no one lived alone. There were no single people as we know them today; unmarried people lived in one household or another. In terms of personal, day-by-day benefits, there may have been little difference between a family member and a household dweller. The only distinction was in terms of inheritance and authority.

Jesus speaks of the household in these terms, where servants and slaves are as integral to the household as the family (Matthew 10:24–25; 24:45–51). Similarly, we read of households being baptized (Acts 16:15; 1 Corinthians 1:16) and of Christian households (Philippians 4:22; 2 Timothy 4:19). Galatians 6:10 speaks of doing good to those who are of the 'household of faith' (although most modern translations replace the word 'household' with 'family'), and Ephesians 2:19 speaks of Christians being 'members of God's household'.

There are therefore two separate but connected images being used in the New Testament:

- The image of family that describes birth, inheritance and authority. This image underlines both the fatherhood of God (Ephesians 3:15) and the inheritance of the new children (3:6) who take their family name from Christ. God the Father is head of this family (with all its implications of ultimate authority).
- The household of faith, which describes the extended family along with their servants (and others) who come under the authority of the father.

Looking at how the early church interpreted these images on a day-to-day basis, we see them doing so in line with their own cultural expectations. Entry into the Christian family came by (new) birth, not choice (John 3:3–8), and this is exactly how the early Christians in Acts behaved—as if they were related to each other (Acts 2:45–47). To express this more precisely, they behaved as if they were of the same household, taking responsibility for one another.

FAMILY AND HOUSEHOLD AS A LEADERSHIP MODEL

In New Testament thought, no member of either the family or the household carried personal authority; that belonged to the father alone. Tasks might be undertaken on his behalf, but only at his command and according to his direction. Personal freedom did not exist for anyone but the father. Everyone else belonged to the family (or household) and worked productively on behalf of the community. To put it bluntly, even beloved sons and servants shared a life of service (Luke 15:28–29).

It is, of course, possible to extrapolate a church leadership model from these New Testament attitudes. The 'sons, servants, slaves' and so forth can be shuffled into some sort of hierarchy, which is then equated to contemporary leadership roles. This was not done by New Testament writers, however. In their thinking, everyone was a child, a servant or a slave. All three terms are used to describe Christians, but they are never juxtaposed. In other words, everyone was a child, or everyone was a servant, or everyone was a slave (or all three at once). Never do the New Testament writers give some Christians the rank of 'child' while others are allocated the rank of 'servant', while yet others are allocated the rank of 'slave'. They simply did not define church leadership in family or household terms. With the exceptions of 1 Thessalonians 2:11–12 (where Paul reminds the church that he always encouraged them in a fatherly way towards God) and 1 Timothy 5:1 (where Timothy is advised to give older men the same respect that he would give his father), every other New Testament reference is to Christians being children together or brothers and sisters.

What is seen in the lives of the early Christians is that they lived in this sibling relationship. Paul regarded the other apostles as brothers, and members of the churches in the same way (in Corinth, Ephesus and everywhere else). Neither he nor any other leader is distinguished as a 'father', 'uncle' or even 'elder brother'. When we look at the images of family or household, what we see is

Christians who have a clear view of their sibling similarity. They are, as it were, in the same circle around their heavenly Father. The New Testament is distorted if these images are used to establish a pattern of leadership, and it is stretched until it snaps when it is presumed that a 21st-century 'family and home' is identical to the first-century 'family and household'.

In our society, the heart of a nuclear family in a contemporary home is seen in terms of social interaction and personal fulfilment (how we get on with each other and individual development). The New Testament model of family and household is quite different from this because it is concerned with authority and community (obedience to the father and sacrificing personal needs for the benefit of others). If, therefore, leadership is thought of in family terms and patterned after the fashion of our contemporary ideas, the main focus of the church tends to become 'getting on with each other and personal development'. The living witness to new life in Christ then starts to look very similar to every other club or interest group, and the church tends to be ignored by non-members, who find friends and personal fulfilment elsewhere.

To Christians in New Testament times, the images of family and household described their relationship with God and their needful service to each other and the world. For us, CM can provide a matrix in which to develop the sibling-like, self-giving love for which Christians have always been known (John 13:34–35). In CM, we are family together in a non-hierarchical way because we all (ordained or lay, minister or member) acknowledge the authority of the same heavenly Father, and the same Holy Spirit active in us all.

In terms of church leadership, there is only one biblical lesson in the imagery of the household of faith and the Christian family: God is in charge.

Chapter 8

THE BRIDE OF CHRIST

The Bible uses the image of marriage to describe the loving relationship between God and his people, and this imagery is very powerful. It contains elements of authority, acceptance and covenant and it is 'interactive' in that we can start from either end in order to understand the other. What we learn about the 'God and us' relationship sheds light on the 'person-to-person' relationship of marriage, and what we learn from marriage helps us to understand our 'God and us' relationship. This brings us back to Genesis 1:26a, where God said, 'Let us make human beings in our image, in our likeness': by looking at human beings we learn something about God, and by looking at God we learn something about ourselves. This interactive process, however, is knocked out of focus by the fall (Genesis 3). Because God is sinless, we may still look at him and learn the truth about ourselves, but because human beings are sinful, care is needed to ensure that human imperfections are not projected on to God.

In recent years, marriage has been popularly used to describe the relationship between God and the church—usually through the image of the 'Bride of Christ'. There has been a tendency, however, to do the theology of the Bride of Christ from a human perspective. Taking a contemporary view of human marriage and using it to describe the church's relationship with God encourages error. Inadvertently, values may be imposed upon God that do not properly belong to him, resulting in a false understanding of who God is, what he is like and what a new covenant relationship with him means. Not to put too fine a point on it, if a fallen human experience is projected on to God, human passions and failings are ascribed to him and God becomes 'made in *our* image and likeness'. By comparison, learning the truth about God and applying that truth to our own relationships is life-giving, and we thus fulfil the purpose of our creation by being 'in the image and likeness' of God.

The image of the Bride of Christ has shaped the understanding of many Christians during their early years of faith formation, which means that many Christian ministers hold a theology of church based in part (and in some cases, in large part) on the following interpretation:

- The church is the bride.
- Christ is the husband.
- The relationship between the two is one of tender, intimate love.

The fact that marriage is used as a metaphor for the relationship between God and his people in both the Old and New Testaments is not in question. In this chapter, however, the meaning of the biblical image will be explored and recent popular interpretations of the metaphor questioned. This may come as something of a shock if we have been taught marriage from the standpoint of contemporary culture rather than from the scriptures,[1] and, if our theology of marriage (filtered through contemporary views) has also been applied to an understanding of church leadership, we may find that we have embraced a cultural rather than biblical structure.

This chapter will consider the nature of the church as it is in the present, and a future for us to look forward to—recognizing that problems arise when the future is confused with the present.

Bride of Christ imagery has been so widely used that it has almost become a nickname for the contemporary church. An example of the kind of passage used in this teaching is Isaiah 62:5: 'As a young man marries a maiden, so will your sons marry you; as a bridegroom rejoices over his bride, so will your God rejoice over you.' It sounds like a straightforward passage about love, tenderness and intimacy, but there are three difficulties with the way in which this passage (and others) have been interpreted. First, present-day assumptions are brought to the text; second, the relationship is defined as if it is present, not future; and third, the result is that the church is expected to be perfect now.

PRESENT-DAY ASSUMPTIONS BROUGHT TO THE TEXT

In our Western culture, as a bride approaches her wedding she probably has certain expectations and concerns:

- She expects an intimate friendship with her husband.
- She expects to be loved, respected and considered.
- She expects to be satisfied in bed.
- She may expect to continue her career and expect her husband to share the household duties.
- She may demand a high level of personal independence in her financial affairs and leisure pursuits.
- She may (or may not) plan to have children.
- She may also have reservations about unresolved areas of life that make future divorce a real possibility.

In a similar fashion, as a groom approaches his wedding he will also probably have expectations and concerns:

- He expects his wife to be his friend.
- He is looking for love, respect and affirmation.
- He expects her to meet his sexual needs and will want to meet hers.
- He may expect his wife to work to support their lifestyle, and may be ready to share the chores with her.
- He may also expect a high level of independence.
- Decisions about children may already be agreed.

- For him (if things don't work out), divorce in the future may be a distinct possibility.

This is how an impending marriage may look to 21st-century eyes, so, when reading the Bible, the tendency may be to interpret the text with 21st-century views. If this happens, a 'marriage relationship' with God may well be regarded as potentially unstable (mirroring an attitude towards contemporary human marriage). Perhaps God will let us down or leave us. Perhaps we will discover that God is not who we think he is and we shall leave him. Perhaps we expect to 'be married' to God but retain a high degree of independence. Perhaps we expect him to meet our needs—on the understanding that if he doesn't, then we may legitimately walk away from him. If a relationship with God is approached in this way, intimacy will probably be emphasized to compensate for potential instability. We will underline how much God loves his people, how sacrificially he gives to human beings, how fundamental his friendship is and how intimate a relationship with him can be. This highly personal interpretation accords with a contemporary approach to marriage because our culture believes that if the love and friendship between husband and wife are strong enough, then whatever other pressures are experienced, the marriage will last.

By treating the biblical metaphor in this way, the theology has been done back to front, imposing a cultural understanding of marriage on to the 'marriage' relationship between God and his people. The problem is that these assumptions are not those of the Bible.

Biblical assumptions

Both the Old and New Testaments reflect a very different culture from our own. When the image of marriage is used in the Bible, it is addressing issues other than those of our expectations today. The way into exploring these biblical concerns is to ask, 'If I lived in Israel in the first century AD (or before), what would my expectations of marriage have been?' We may not be sure exactly what that culture was like, but it was similar in many significant ways to cultures in the rural Third World and in the Near East today. Fundamental to the biblical image of marriage is the absolute authority of the husband. So, when a bride from this kind of culture approaches her wedding, her concerns and expectations are probably along these lines.

- She hopes that her father has chosen her husband wisely.
- She hopes for a gentle husband who will respect her.
- She yearns for love and hopes to be loved.
- She expects a breadwinner and hopes for security, if not wealth.
- She expects to obey her husband.
- She expects to give him children.
- She expects to take her place in the society of married women, especially the circle of her husband's female kin.

The groom also, as he approaches his wedding, has expectations and concerns:

- He too hopes that his parents have chosen a good wife for him.
- He hopes to be adored, but will settle for submissiveness.
- If there is a 'love void', so be it. Regardless, he expects complete faithfulness from his wife.
- If no children arrive, he will possibly divorce her and remarry, or take a second wife.
- He expects his wife to manage his home and children while he makes money.
- He will spend most of his leisure time in the company of other men, and his male in-laws will expect him to include them in his business dealings.

It helps, therefore, to recognize that in Jesus' time (and before), the image of marriage emphasized arrangement, security, obedience, submissiveness, hope and even ownership. There was also a fundamental expectation that both husband and wife would join a larger, extended family network. In some ways, drawing conclusions about God from this understanding of marriage also runs the risk of doing the theology back to front. Therefore, it is unwise to draw conclusions, for example, about male headship from this particular cultural understanding. The point in the context of this book, however, is this: writers in the Old and New Testaments found the metaphor of marriage useful because, according to their understanding, it emphasized the authority of God.

Our attitude to marriage today is largely individualistic. To us, marriage is about the happiness of the bride and groom. They are the centre of attention on their wedding day and their continued love is held to be the primary reason for their union. In the culture of the Bible, the expectations were largely corporate. Marriage was about having children and contributing to the community. Although fêted on the wedding day, the joining of the families was as important as the joining of the couple. In the long term, happiness and love between husband and wife were hoped for, but faithfulness was more important. In the Bible, the metaphor of marriage between God and his people needs to be viewed with all these overtones of obedience and submission on our part and of lordship on God's part. The corporate nature of marriage should also be recognized, as individuals join not just a husband or wife, but a new family (the household of faith).

As we look at other Bible passages with these emphases in mind, interpretation becomes straightforward, even when the human relationship values expressed do not sit comfortably with our own cultural opinions.

- Isaiah 49:18 describes children (God's people) as both a possession and a glorious adornment.

- Isaiah 61:10 refers to the groom (the Messiah) in priestly terms, while the bride (the people) is valued for her beauty.
- In Luke 5:33–35, when Jesus is challenged about the behaviour of his disciples, he uses wedding imagery to answer his critics. His disciples are feasting the bridegroom (Jesus). As an aside, it should be noted that from our perspective we live in the fasting time (v. 35).
- In John 3:27–30, John the Baptist refers to himself as the groom's friend. In our culture, the nearest thing we have to this is the 'best man'. John is quite clear that he, like a best man, will diminish when the groom (Jesus) arrives to claim his bride (God's people).
- In Revelation 21:2–4, Jerusalem is prepared in heaven as a bride and then presented to her husband. The husband (whose identity is not stated here, but can be extrapolated from Revelation 19:7–9) is Christ.
- In Revelation 22:17, the Spirit and the bride welcome the groom, and all are invited to join in the welcome, which brings life.

All of these passages have been used as a basis for Bride of Christ teaching, but with little reference to the biblical context. In this way, the image has been used to bolster a view of the 'God and church' relationship that is not biblically tenable. When interpreted through the filter of our own culture, the image becomes one of intimate personal relationship, and some worship songs (which teach doctrine by default) have been particularly guilty of this kind of cultural spin by describing the relationship between 'bride and groom' in nigh-on sexual terms.

By reading these Bible passages with an appropriate cultural understanding of marriage, some wonderful truths about God can be learnt. He is loving, forgiving and willing to set aside his 'rights' in order to better the life of his bride. Astonishingly, he is a 'husband' who refuses to 'demand' of his bride; instead, he moves heaven and earth for her benefit. In the final analysis, though, the Bible is reminding us that he is our ultimate authority.

DEFINING THE RELATIONSHIP IN THE PRESENT DAY

The second difficulty with these texts is that they may have been used to describe the new covenant relationship between God and his church as it is experienced in the present. If fact, however, these passages do not describe a present reality: they describe a work in progress and a future promise. The biblical image of the bride always refers to the future, not to the present. The picture is always of the apocalyptic church, the future Jerusalem (meaning the central gathering of God's own people), made perfect and acceptable to be the bride.

The Bride of Christ is therefore an image of something that *will* happen. It is neither a picture of what has already happened nor a description of what is happening now. If the image has been misinterpreted to describe the church in the present, expectations about what the church is like will probably be skewed. When the Bible uses the image of marriage to describe God's *present* relationship with his people, it uses husband and wife, not bride and groom. Jesus is the groom who will take his bride at the future judgment; when speaking of the present relationship, the Bible refers to God as a husband.

Ignoring the husband...

Because recent teaching has tended to concentrate only on the bride and groom, it has often ignored the passages that refer to the husband. Let's look at some representative passages.

- Hosea 1:2: The prophet is told to marry an adulterous wife. Their marriage is the symbol of Israel's unfaithfulness.
- Jeremiah 3:6–13: Here the idolatrous people are described as an adulterous wife.
- Joel 1:8: The people are told to mourn like an unfulfilled widow.
- Mark 8:38: Jesus refers to the unbelief of the people as adultery.

The main point to note is that passages which use marriage to describe a present relationship between God and his people always speak in terms of the wife's unfaithfulness. This 'adultery' refers to the worship of other gods (idolatry), and might be thought of as an entirely Hebrew or old covenant problem. In fact, Paul refers to idolatry as a current problem in his day (for example, Galatians 4:8) along with the tendency for Christians to turn to it (4:9). Applied to the people of God in both covenants, these passages expect the 'wife' to be, above all else, faithful.

The imagery of bride and wife

When we look at these Bible passages together, we may find that we have something unexpected to chew on.

- Passages about marriage are to do with the Lordship of God.
- Passages about the husband refer to the adultery of the people of God (in the present).
- Passages about the bride refer to the future state of the church when it is (we are) finally sanctified.
- These attitudes and imagery are summed up in Ephesians 5:25–28, where Paul speaks of Christ lovingly preparing the church for the forthcoming wedding.

It does seem, then, that the image of the Bride of Christ has been somewhat misunderstood in recent years. It has been used to promote the church as a place of intimacy with God, whereas, in both Old and New Testament terms, intimacy in marriage is not a bridal expectation. If it is present, then it is a happy by-product of obedience, fertility and a husband who turns out to be wonderful!

Isaiah 54:4–5 refers to this issue of cultural expectation. Here, the people of God are described as both an abandoned, barren wife and a widow bereft of her husband. Just as the young bride of that time hoped for a kind, forgiving husband, so we hope that God will be like this. Just as the widow longs for her loneliness to cease, so we hope that God will meet us and take us under his Lordship. How delightful to find that he is indeed a loving, forgiving 'husband' who draws us to himself, to save us and rule us!

THE RESULT OF MISUNDERSTANDING THE IMAGERY

As individual Christians, we rejoice that through Christ we are counted as righteous in spite of our sin (like Abraham: Romans 3:21–24; 4:3, 22–25), and that we live in a state of tension between what has been, what is and what will be. As Paul says, in the past we have sinned but, because of the cross of Christ, God regards us as righteous. In the future, at judgment, this sanctification will be completed, but right here, right now, we both sin and are regarded as righteous at the same time. We are not yet perfect (Philippians 3:12) and yet we are (Hebrews 10:14)! As individuals, then, we are used to thinking in terms of this personal paradox.

If the Bride of Christ imagery is applied to the church according to our culture, however, this paradox disappears and the 'righteous' aspect of Christian life becomes overemphasized. The church is thought to exist primarily to facilitate an intimate relationship with God, and, when the image is used to describe the church now rather than in the future, the church may be expected to be already perfect—when it clearly isn't! As a by-product, this can shape our view of leadership because, if the church is both intimate with God and perfect, then its leaders should be too. The logic is that if these are the qualities of the church, then the top man must, of all people, exhibit them himself. This in turn connects with two facets of contemporary culture: pyramidal leadership and achievement.

First of all, in the secular world the successful are promoted—usually to the point where they stop succeeding; they then tend to stick at that level for the remainder of their career. Those who occupy middle layers of leadership are reasonably safe because, if something goes wrong, the failure may attach to someone below or above them. The man at the top, though, like the man at the bottom, is allowed no failure. If he or his organization fails, he resigns. This is because, in a pyramid, the pinnacle leader is in ultimate charge: he not only gives the orders, he also accepts the responsibility.

Secondly, our culture values achievement—in contrast to the Bible, which values obedience. In order to think about achievement and obedience, let's ask a question. If a mother sends her son to buy a bag of beans from the local shop, is the boy regarded as obedient when he heads for the door or only when he brings the beans back? In biblical terms, the boy is obedient as soon he begins the task (even if he fails to complete it). In our culture, we tend to think of obedience as 'completing the task'. Therefore, if the boy fails to return with the beans, his failure is regarded as disobedience (and he will probably find it necessary to invent all sorts of excuses in order to avoid blame).

If we have come to expect perfection in the church, the most usual sign of this is the expectation of success. If failure is not an option, the consequence tends to be that bad situations and difficult circumstances are reinterpreted as successes. The easiest way to describe this is to comment on a joke:

Q: How many ministers does it take to change a light bulb?
A: None, because if you look *very* carefully you'll see that the old bulb is still working.

Comment: The light is still shining even though no one can see it. The minister hasn't failed—what a relief!

The recent interpretation of Bride of Christ imagery has given credence to cultural, success-based leadership (the pyramid) because the image bolsters the idea of church perfection. It is a short step from there to seeing the concepts of both present and future judgment by God disappear altogether. The final step is for membership of the church (already the bride) to be regarded as tantamount to an entry ticket into heaven. More than this, if the image is reinterpreted according to our own cultural expectations, we may end up with a false view of church and demand success rather than obedience from all leaders (while also, by default, setting them up for a fall). Everyone is then destined for disillusionment, because the church will consistently disappoint; it will never live up to the false promise.

By contrast, the biblical image for the current covenant relationship (unfaithful wife) shows that God does not expect the church to be either perfect or successful in all things. Church, in the present, just isn't like that—it's much more likely to be disloyal than perfect. What applies to the church also applies to church leaders. God expects repentance and obedience—and ministers should take a lead in this (Romans 7:15–25).

A repentant wife?

If the images of wife and bride are understood in the biblical sense, both ministers and members can be properly enthusiastic about the future—and absolutely realistic about the present, This helps everyone to be honest and may well lead to questions such as:

- Has the church been unfaithful to God? If we have, in what ways have we been unfaithful?
- In what ways are we being prepared as the bride?
- When we undertake church activities, who are we trying to please?

Ephesians 4:1–6 may be helpful here because it reminds us that working at being church is a worthy response to God's actions and presence. The image of the church as a wife is a reminder that unfaithfulness is nothing new, while the image of the bride proclaims what God has done, and will do, for his church. It underscores that all Christians are in the same position, and it assures us of what our loving God has prepared for the future. It also helps us to understand that the church is far from perfect, and encourages us to endure its failings.

The consequence of realizing that the church is an unfaithful wife while, paradoxically, also being prepared as a future bride is that our understanding of leadership is adjusted. Because this imagery underlines the authority of God as both the groom and the husband, ministers and leaders are enabled to occupy a non-hierarchical place beside every other Christian in the church. Their leadership and personal gifts are important to the church, but they in themselves are no more or less significant than any other person, and the personal relationship that each person has with Jesus Christ is the basis for collaboration with each other.

This means, for example, that collaborative leaders are able to admit to both success and failure. 'Falling short' is a way of life for the wife, not an exceptional circumstance, and when it is recognized that ministry belongs to the whole church (a shared priesthood), it becomes straightforward for even the minister to admit that his area of ministry isn't going very well. Failure is no longer a resigning issue because everyone falls short, and everyone has a long way to go. Similarly, it becomes possible to accept the fact that the bulb needs changing—and to get a completely new lamp or even rewire the whole house if necessary. When Christians work collaboratively, difficult circumstances and problems can be admitted openly, and personal fault becomes the starting place for change.

NOTE

1 For a detailed study of marriage in the Bible, refer to *Marriage—Restoring Our Vision*.

Chapter 9

A SPIRITUAL TEMPLE

In the past, Collaborative Ministry has been called 'enabling ministry' but, strictly speaking, the two are not the same. Previously, the phrase 'enabling' tended to mean that the minister enables the people of his church to minister (and the key phrase is 'his church'). When a church is thought of as being the minister's church, authority is vested in him. He may 'enable' members to minister, but the pyramid remains. In CM, the meaning is that the Holy Spirit enables the people to minister under the authority of Christ. Having established that the Spirit collaborates with the church in ministry, and that Christ is indeed the one high priest, the head of the household, the husband and the groom, it's time to focus on 'acceptance' or membership. In the epistles, the image of the spiritual temple is used to help Christians to understand the work of the Spirit in the church.

An understanding of temple worship follows on from an understanding of priesthood, and together these concepts tend to shape our theology of church. This, in turn, defines an understanding of leadership and, by default, the attitude to church members. In terms of CM, the image of a spiritual temple makes it clear that church is not primarily an activity in which human beings engage, but a creative action of God. It is therefore not a description of what to do, but of how to be. If the church is the 'new temple', it then assumes the functions of the old temple and becomes the place where God is worshipped, known and met—and where the Ten Commandments are kept. The question for us to ask is this: will every expression of the new temple (each church) look exactly the same as every other?

THE TEMPLE

In the old covenant, priests exercised their priesthood in the temple. The two were so inextricably linked that when the third temple was destroyed in AD70, the priesthood, in effect, ceased to be. As we have already seen, in the new covenant, priesthood was ascribed to the church, and this chapter can be thought of as the second part of Chapter 6. In the same way that the old covenant concepts of priesthood and temple were linked, so too, in the new covenant, the 'priesthood of all believers' is inextricably linked to the concept of the church as a spiritual temple.

A good place to begin is by playing the children's game 'Here's the church'. Remember that? Clasp hands together, fingers tucked inside and thumbs side by side: 'Here's the church... and here's the steeple...' (raise forefingers) 'open the doors...' (thumbs apart) 'and see the people!' (open hands back to back, fingers still interlaced, and wiggle fingers). Interestingly, this game expresses a significant theology. The church building turns into the people, or, to put it another way, the church *is* the people, and both of them are made up from one body. Chapter 10 explores what it means to be the 'body of Christ' but here the focus is on the church as a spiritual temple. In the children's game, it is impossible to form the church without the fingers, which are the people. In New Testament theology, it is impossible to form a spiritual temple without a holy priesthood of all believers—and vice versa.

Now let's look at some key passages, starting with 1 Peter 2:4–5: 'As you come to him, the living Stone—rejected by men but chosen by God and precious to him—you also, like living stones, are being built into a spiritual house to be a holy priesthood, offering spiritual sacrifices acceptable to God through Jesus Christ.'

In these verses there are four elements that help to form a complete image of the 'spiritual house', which, by virtue of its sacrificial content and priesthood, is a temple. Those elements are the keystone, the Commandments, the new covenant temple, and the diverse stones.

THE KEYSTONE

In John 2:19 Jesus refers to himself as the temple. Although misunderstood and mocked at the time, he was speaking prophetically about his death and resurrection (vv. 21–22). When he made this statement, Jesus was standing in the outer temple court with the remnants of the market scattered around him (vv. 14–16). This outer court, which was also known as the Court of the Gentiles, was the place where believers like Cornelius (Acts 10:1–2) might come to pray. Jesus had routed the traders because he objected to them using the space for commercial purposes: in his opinion, every court in the temple should be a place where people might come and meet with God.

The temple signified the dwelling of God among his people. Originally, the tablets inscribed with the Ten Commandments were kept in the ark of the covenant, in the Holy of Holies. Also, it was in the temple that sacrifices were made and sin was dealt with. In John 2:19–21, Jesus predicted his own destruction with the affirmation that he would build 'the temple' again in three days. This implied a new Holy of Holies, somewhere to keep the Commandments, a sacrifice to atone for sin, and a place for God to dwell. So there would still be a temple (and only one temple) but it would no longer be located in Jerusalem.

Let's briefly consider three of the things Jesus said about himself:

- He would fulfil the Commandments (Matthew 5:17–20).
- He would offer himself as a sacrifice (Matthew 16:21).
- To know him is to know God (John 8:19; 14:9–10).

All of these statements carry temple implications, which can be summed up in one word: 'Emmanuel' ('God with us'). In the incarnation of Christ there is more than the perfect image of God in human form (Genesis 1:27): there is, in him, a new Holy of Holies as God is met in a person, not a place (John 20:28). Jesus is also the sacrifice and the great high priest, but he was always the 'meeting place' where God dwelt among his people (John 1:14). In the new, spiritual temple, Jesus is the Gentile court, the women's court, the men's court, the altar of sacrifice and the Holy of Holies—and in him, the Commandments are realized.

In this new temple, built from living stones, Jesus is the most important stone (Matthew 21:42). The spiritual temple will replace the temple of the old covenant (v. 43) and those who reject it will destroy themselves (v. 44). Because the temple and the priesthood were interlinked, Jesus' listeners knew exactly what he was talking about (v. 45). 1 Peter 2:6–8 also refers to Jesus as the 'cornerstone' or 'stumbling block'. For the church, this means that unless Jesus is the keystone, then the church cannot be a spiritual temple.

The new temple is a work of God through Jesus Christ in the power of the Spirit: 'Consequently, you are no longer foreigners and aliens, but fellow citizens with God's people and members of God's household, built on the foundation of the apostles and prophets, with Christ Jesus himself as the chief cornerstone. In him the whole building is joined together and rises to become a holy temple to the Lord. And in him you too are being built together to become a dwelling in which God lives by his Spirit' (Ephesians 2:19–22). The new temple is founded on, and held together by, Jesus. During the three years of his ministry, he in his own person was the 'place' where God dwelt with his people and where God might be met. Now, the church is where God dwells and the lives of Christians are the living stones that are built upon the lives of the apostles and prophets to form the new spiritual temple. The place where God dwells and may be met is the church: here it is, and here's the steeple… now open the doors and see the people… because these lives are the new dwelling place of God.

THE COMMANDMENTS

The Ten Commandments were written on two tablets of stone (Exodus 31:18). These sacred objects were carried through the wilderness and into the promised land before coming to rest in the innermost sanctum of the temple. There was, however, a prophetic promise linked to them (Ezekiel 36:26–27; Jeremiah 31:33). Disobedient, stubborn, 'stony' hearts would one day be replaced with obedient hearts, filled with the life of God's Holy Spirit and testament to the Commandments. In the fulfilment of this prophecy, the Commandments would no longer be carved in stone and laid to rest in the temple; instead, they would live in the hearts of the obedient people of God. This promise is not about effort, but about the presence of the Holy Spirit; it is not about what God's people must do, but about what God will do for his people. It will be fulfilled when the Spirit of God enlivens human hearts so that human beings live the law. In Chapter 5, we saw that this 'enlivening of the Spirit' was experienced at Pentecost, and continues in the church today.

Christians are living stones, and the Commandments of God are written on human lives. The new temple therefore still contains the Commandments in its inner sanctum, but this time the sacred inner place is the hearts of believers. In terms of 1 Peter 2:5, Christian lives are now 'living tablets' upon which the law of God is written and made known. Just as in the old covenant temple, these tablets, or stones, are to be found in the new temple, which is the spiritual gathering of believers called the church.

THE TEMPLE—AND THE NEW COVENANT TEMPLE

The first temple was built by Solomon (1 Kings 6) as a holy place where God dwelt among the people, where the stone tablets of the Commandments were kept, and where all sacrifices for sin were made. There was only one temple, and yet God promised his people an abiding temple under the kingship of the Messiah (Ezekiel 37:25–28). Once again, the New Testament image is of Christian lives being built, like living stones, into this spiritual temple. Built upon and depending on the cornerstone of Christ, it is the living embodiment of the law of God. The new temple is as visible as the old temple and it fulfils the same remit.

This means that Christians, together, are the holy place of God's dwelling (1 Corinthians 3:16–17), where the Commandments are kept and where sin is dealt with. It is clear that being church is a corporate activity, that it is not a man-made construction and that it is a spiritual reality. In New Testament terms, 'church' had nothing to do with buildings and everything to do with a gathering of living stones built upon the one cornerstone—Jesus Christ.

In God's remarkable economy, this new covenant temple can be achieved with a very small gathering: according to Jesus, two or three will do (Matthew 18:20). Therefore, two or three Christians going out in ministry are just as much church as hundreds of Christians meeting together for worship. In the old covenant, the temple was the religious centre that drew in every worshipper. The new covenant temple, by comparison, is still the religious centre, but now God's people focus outwards from it. The church is not centralist, but centred and expanding. Whereas the hallmarks of the old covenant were strict adherence to specific patterns of behaviour and worship, the hallmarks of the new covenant are freedom and diversity.

A DIVERSITY OF STONES

If we are asked to picture a stone block, the chances are that we will think of an elongated cube, like a brick but bigger. Therefore, when the church is pictured as a gathering of 'living stones', there's a tendency to expect that every stone will be the same regular shape. Today, if we look around a stone-built church, we soon discover that there are all sorts of shapes and sizes of stone block used. There are pillar stones that carry or hold the weight and stress of the building. There are flag stones that everyone walks on but few notice. Window stones often bear the brunt of the weather and may be worn or damaged. Every arch will have a keystone. Some stones will be dressed and others will be carved. Within the walls, there will be rubble that strengthens them, unseen. There may be gravestones and memorials. Coping stones provide protection, and of course there are foundation stones. To build with stone, diversity is needed, because each stone does a different job.

If Christians are living stones, built into a spiritual temple, then perhaps these stones can be related to ministry. It may be a fruitful exercise to make a list of all the different types of stone that make a church building, and relate each one to a different ministry. It's a straightforward task and a useful way of looking at CM: to make up a single building, there must be different elements. We should also remember that there is a mutual task for each living stone: to build one another up in the faith (Jude 20–23).

Thinking of stones as conforming to a regular, similar pattern may indicate a tendency towards 'replication' in the church. In one sense, this is a proper process because every Christian bears a similarity to Christ (Romans 8:29). It is also appropriate for Christians to learn from the example of others (1 Corinthians 11:1)—although there is a rider to this: Paul does not say, 'Be like me'; he says, 'Be like me in as much as I am like Christ.' Therefore, when Christians learn from the holiness and faith of others, it is beneficial because by 'following' them we are following the one whom they follow—Christ. If we fashion our lives in the image of others' ministry, however, we may attempt to shape our own stone in the likeness of theirs, and this is not a proper process.

The New Testament expects every 'living stone' to be filled with the Holy Spirit. As a consequence, each person will have gifts to offer (1 Corinthians 12:7), but these gifts are as diverse as the stones that make up a building, and all are needed if the structure is to fulfil its intended purpose. There are two aspects to this work of the Holy Spirit:

- Christian lives produce spiritual fruit (Galatians 5:22–23).
- Spiritual gifts are given (Romans 12; 1 Corinthians 12).

An in-depth study of spiritual fruit and spiritual gifts (and the specific differences between them) would be a diversion here, but it is useful to establish a rule of thumb. Spiritual fruit grow in Christian lives for the purpose of personal holiness. Spiritual gifts are given to be used in the church, and through the church, for the benefit of others. The fact that a Christian is 'gifted' says nothing about his or her personal holiness.

Thinking about this in terms of ministry, we can see how traditional pyramidal leadership and CM diverge. The hierarchical pyramid tends to produce uniformity in leadership; CM tends to produce distinctive ministries that take everyone by surprise. In CM, the living stones are expected to be diverse. The shape of the spiritual temple does not prescribe the shape of the stones; rather, the stones dictate the shape of the temple. In CM, the fruit in every church will be the same, but the gifts and the shape of the stones will cause diversity in structure and task.

A WARNING

According to 2 Thessalonians 2:3–4, the new temple will be the place where 'the man of lawlessness' will exalt himself. This is an apocalyptic vision referring to the second coming of Christ, before which 'the man' will try to divide and rule. In verse 7, however, the apostle reminds the Thessalonian church that this 'secret power' is already at work among them. The epistles reveal that the early church (the new, spiritual temple) was far from perfect (a wife, yet to become the bride)—with power struggles, sexual immorality and heretical teaching. In most of our contemporary churches, we shall from time to time be faced with these painful, divisive behaviours, but on a daily basis we are much more likely to be faced with lying accusation (which is retitled 'gossip'). When this happens, it bears the hallmark of 'the man of lawlessness' and requires action.

The word 'gossip' tends to be used to sanitize the truth, which is that words become like stones, which are flung at the accused in their absence. Gossip kills reputations and destroys a person's standing with God in the church. Gossip is usually unverified accusation, and it is often what the Bible calls 'false witness'. True witnesses verify with the person concerned (Matthew 18:15–17) because they are motivated by a desire to build up (Jude 20), whereas the desire of 'the man of lawlessness' is to pull down. According to the new covenant, Jesus has taken all sin upon himself (Romans 6:10). Christians, therefore, have no business judging others (Matthew 7:1), let alone stoning them! Those who live in spiritual temples shouldn't throw stones.

Building a spiritual temple is a work of God, not human beings. Because a CM structure encourages a very large number of people to express their opinions, care is needed to make sure that opinion does not twist into gossip. Therefore, it is important for any CM church to establish a communication process that differentiates between the voice of God and the voice of lawlessness.

BEING, NOT DOING

If the New Testament imagery of the spiritual temple is used as a template for a leadership structure, the contemporary church will do something that the New Testament itself does not do. If leadership roles and functions are overlaid on to this temple imagery, the resulting structure does not fit with New Testament values. In the early church, the apostles were very careful to point out the difference between the old and new temples, and there was much rejoicing that the old temple had been replaced by a new temple built from Christian hearts and lives.

There are two clear messages from the New Testament image of the new covenant temple:

- It is not a pattern for leadership; it is a description of what God has done, and is doing, in the heart of every believer. It is about being, not doing.
- A group of Christians founded on Christ is a temple (or church); a gathering of Christians around a high-profile individual is not.

Pyramidal leadership is the antithesis of the spiritual temple because it focuses on, and from, the individual at the top. CM recognizes Jesus Christ as the one pinnacle leader, and shares roles and functions according to gifting. The aim and practice of the church is to be built into a spiritual structure where the priesthood of Christ is exercised.

HOMOGENY AND DIVERSITY

Our culture, for a variety of reasons, tends to homogenize. It is not only shopping centres in every town and city that look remarkably similar—so do churches. As a consequence, vision, leadership training, expectation of results and so forth tend to be standardized. In some ways this is helpful because it allows good practice to be shared, but in one significant way it creates a problem. Standardization only works when the raw materials used, or the products sold, are identical. Homogeny only works across communities where there is a consistency of attitude and experience. In church terms, this means that each individual church must provide the same 'shape' of living stone and build a living temple that accords with a notional, national (or international) blueprint.

With priesthood this is possible, because there is only one high priest (Christ himself) so there is only one blueprint for redemption (more about this in Chapter 11). When it comes to church membership, however, every living stone is different, and each collection of living stones (church) is different from every other. This being the case, ministry will vary too. Pyramidal leadership solves this problem from the top down by shaping the church according to the leadership. CM solves the problem from the bottom up by shaping the leadership according to the church. Leaders and ministers are vital because they are distinctive stones, and their ministry can perhaps be thought of in terms of 'columns' or 'arch stones', without which the church would collapse. The central issue, therefore, is not about whether ministers are necessary (they are, regardless of the leadership style), but about whether their task is to shape the church according to an imposed pattern or to encourage the church to build something unique with the available materials. Pyramidal leadership seeks the former; CM seeks the latter.

Collaborative Ministry as a style of leadership remains constant wherever it is applied, but the results of CM are different in every church. This means that in a culture committed to homogeny, CM enables, encourages and rejoices in diversity. Because it is a bottom-up structure, with the leadership being shaped by its membership, it is accessible to the community that it serves. Pyramidal structures tend to take the 'top people' as their reference point and can therefore be suspicious of those who prefer not to conform or are, as yet, inexperienced in the church. At worst, this can mean that all ministers are imported and that only very select local people are allowed into leadership. If these people are culturally, educationally and experientially different from the community that the church serves, the leadership may seem remote to non-members. Because CM seeks to recognize gifting, it takes the 'bottom people' in the church as its reference point, expecting to find gifts of leadership that can be encouraged and trained. Because these leaders are necessarily from the same cultural background as the rest of the community, this may make the church more accessible to non-members. It also means that the church can do more than offer membership: it can offer the possibility of becoming a leader and sharing in a wide variety of ministry.

CM reverses the children's game by playing it inside out. 'Here are the people, here's the church...' and it's a living, spiritual temple where the Commandments are kept, where Christ is both the sacrifice and the high priest, and where, in the hearts and lives of Christian people, God dwells and might be met.

Chapter 10

THE BODY OF CHRIST

'The body of Christ' is one of the most familiar images used to describe the church. In the past, 'every member ministry' (EMM) has often been closely connected with the imagery of 'body ministry'. EMM tends to mean 'every church member doing their bit for the good of the whole'. In a sense, this is similar to New Testament 'body ministry', but it is not identical as there are two significant differences.

First, EMM has most usually been attempted within a pyramidal structure of leadership. Therefore, although every member does their bit, some 'bits' are unarguably more important than others. It may said, for example, that giving out the books on Sunday is every bit as important as preaching, but the contrasting attention given to each activity reveals the real opinion.

Second, EMM has tended to replace gifts with skills. Every church needs skills as well as gifts, but when a church relies on skills alone, anyone who cannot match certain criteria tends to be excluded. This may not matter for the 'giving out the books ministry', where only basic skills are needed, but for 'preaching ministry' and the like, qualifications and literacy become the norm. This tends to knock some people into a 'fit only to follow' category. Gifts are not skills, because skills are developed and trained while gifts are given, but EMM tends to allocate tasks according to a skill level (which will probably be set by those at the pinnacle of leadership).

In EMM there is a tendency to promote rank and value skill. CM, by recognizing Jesus Christ as the head of the body, expects the

Holy Spirit to distribute spiritual gifts throughout the body, and expects every member to receive. Gifts are not ranked and all contribute. Gifting does not depend on literacy, education or self-confidence, and through the exercise of their gifts individuals can overcome negative past experiences. The Spirit of God touches whom he chooses for the benefit of the body, and often calls unlikely people into leadership. The hallmark of EMM is finding people for tasks; the hallmark of CM is figuring out how to help people to use their gifts.

As we consider the image of 'the body of Christ', it's helpful to think of it as following on from the imagery of marriage. Just as, in a human marriage relationship, couples vow to honour one another with their bodies, in similar fashion the church can be described as the body with which Christians honour Christ.

Any mention of bodies brings us back to the foundational concept of incarnation. This is a primary understanding about God—that he chooses to interact with his creation in bodily form. He does not think, create and leave; he speaks, his words take form and he himself enters into his creative statement.

INCARNATION

When we talk about the body of Christ, we usually mean the church. To appreciate the image, though, we also need to think about the body of Christ that was born, drank milk, grew up, walked and talked and was crucified. In this body of flesh and blood, Jesus was God incarnate, God dwelling in flesh, made man (John 1:1–14). Because the incarnation of Christ was a 'once-in-creation event', there is a tendency to think of it as an entirely 'new thing' (Acts 17:19–20), because, in the most significant sense, it was! Jesus inaugurated the new covenant (Luke 22:20), and because of him 'if anyone is in Christ, there is a new creation' (2 Corinthians 5:17). In another sense, though, the incarnation was the fulfilment of the old covenant, and as such it began in the 'same place', repeating and overlaying God's previous creative pattern.

Let's look at some Bible passages. First, in Genesis 1:26–27, God makes human beings in his own image. This is an incarnational statement which asserts that observation of human beings will reveal something of God's character. Similarly, the relationship between the first human beings and God is described in incarnational terms, as the creator 'walks' with the created (Genesis 3:8). Then, in Genesis 12:1–3, God calls Abram to found a new nation. This is to be achieved incarnationally, the chosen couple becoming a family which will grow through descent into a 'people'. In this way, God chooses to interact with the world in an incarnate way, this time through the bodies of Abraham, Sarah and their descendants. Moving to the New Testament, in Luke 1:26–38, an angel announces to Mary that she will become pregnant and bear a child. God is once again choosing to interact with his creation through flesh, in bodily form.

Thus it is clear that there is an incarnational sense to the creation right from the beginning. It is human beings who will 'steward the earth', the people of God in the old covenant (Abraham's descendants) who will 'steward redemption' as a holy priesthood to the nations, and Jesus Christ who 'stewards salvation'. In the epistles, Paul makes this incarnational theme very clear. He recognizes Jesus as the 'new Adam' (Romans 5:12–17) and also links him with Abraham (Romans 4:13–25). Just as Adam was the founder of the race and Abraham the founder of God's holy nation, so Jesus is the founder of both the new race and God's new covenant nation. When Paul draws these comparisons between Jesus and Adam (and Abraham), he is confirming the old covenant but explaining that God has now overlaid these founding fathers with Christ, so that every promise of the old covenant might be fulfilled in the new. The two covenants are not 'end to end', the new one beginning where the old one finished (as if the new were some sort of extension of the old). The new covenant begins in the same place as the old, so it is more like a second storey built on top of the first, covering the same ground but in a new way. Thus the original created order continues: the relationship between God and the human race remains, being restored rather than replaced, and God continues to interact with his creation incarnationally.

This brings us to the church. In the new covenant, the church is the body of Christ in the world (John 14:12). It is the incarnational interaction between God and human beings. As the church 'builds up' disciples, it collaborates with God as he builds relationships with individuals—a task suitable for the race born of the new Adam (Romans 5:17–18). As the church 'goes out', it collaborates with God as he builds relationships with the world—a task appropriate for the children of the new Abraham (Galatians 3:29). Thus the work of Christ becomes the work of the church (2 Corinthians 5:18–21). Just as God related to and through Adam, Abraham, the chosen people and Christ, now he relates to and through the church.

THE BODY OF CHRIST

The image of the body is used in various places in the New Testament. Its existence affirms that Gentiles also receive covenant promises (Ephesians 3:6), because each church, whatever religion its members previously adhered to, is not a 'separate body' but part of the one body of Christ (Ephesians 4:4), which should be ruled by his peace (Colossians 3:15). The image is used most comprehensively, though, in chapter 12 of both Romans and 1 Corinthians.

In Romans 12:4–5, Paul makes three points about the church:

- Each body part has a different function.
- These different functions are united into one body by Christ.
- Because it is one body, each part is connected not only to Christ, but to all the other parts.

In 1 Corinthians 12:12–27, he develops the image by mentioning different parts of the body. He refers to hands and feet (v. 15), ears, eyes and noses (vv. 16–17), and points out that some parts are weaker, less honourable and unpresentable (vv. 22–24). The points he makes here are:

- All body parts are indispensable (v. 14).
- The body is arranged according to God's design (v. 18).
- The body must contain diverse parts to function (vv. 19–21).
- There is no hierarchy (v. 25).
- What affects one part affects the whole (v. 26).
- There are no passengers (v. 27).

When this passage is combined with Romans 12:4–5, we are left with a powerful image of the church—and a reminder of just how difficult it is to function in this way. The temptation is for hands or eyes to regard themselves as superior to feet or ears. Similarly, it is all too easy for every part to aspire to one particular function, but, as Paul points out, such a body would be a monster.

Here, the image refers to the 'building up' aspect of the church's life, but it is also closely connected with 'going out', and this is why both passages refer to spiritual gifts in connection with the body of Christ.

Spiritual gifts

In Romans 12:6–8, Paul mentions the gifts of prophecy, service, teaching, encouraging, giving, leadership and showing mercy. In 1 Corinthians 12:7–10, he mentions messages of wisdom and knowledge, faith, healing, miraculous powers, prophecy, distinguishing between spirits, tongues and the interpretation of tongues. After the 'hymn' of 1 Corinthians 13, he continues in chapter 14 by giving guidelines that explain how to exercise prophecy and tongues appropriately and order worship suitably. Basically, he tells the Corinthian church to grow up (14:20).

While it is useful to examine spiritual gifts in detail, this study focuses on the body, not the parts. We should recognize, however, that Paul, by referring to the gifts, makes it clear that these are elements of ministry that he expects to see in the church. He also expects a variety of people to exercise them, and his guidelines for their use and his instructions for worship paint a picture of the errors into which Corinth fell. To sum up, this was a church that ranked some gifts above others and thereby created a hierarchy that should not exist.

Let's be clear about these passages: they do not rank spiritual gifts or necessarily link them with specific leadership roles. Paul is not writing to the church leaders, but to every member of the church (Romans 1:7; 1 Corinthians 1:2). He regards some gifts as 'greater' than others in that they are key to evangelism (1 Corinthians 12:31; 14:1–40) but he teaches that all gifts should be present and exercised appropriately. If 1 Corinthians 12:28 is interpreted to apply only to ministers, with a 'leadership pyramid' built upon it, we miss the point not only of chapter 12, but also of chapters 13 and 14. Paul says that apostles are 'first', prophets 'second' and teachers 'third', but this is unlikely to mean that they were leadership roles with specific status either in Corinth or the universal church. If this were the case, then Corinth wouldn't need advice on how to exercise gifts or how to order worship: the Corinthian apostle (or, in his absence, the prophet) would just exercise his authority and tell those in error to keep quiet. The fact that this did not happen shows that verse 28 was neither establishing nor addressing a leadership hierarchy. Rather, Paul gives guidance about how to handle spiritual gifts (and the roles of apostle, prophet and teacher) precisely because they are *not* related to a hierarchical leadership structure. In Paul's thinking, the church has only one authority because the body has only one head—Christ.

The first letter of Peter is addressed to churches, not to leaders (1 Peter 1:1), and the same point about spiritual gifts is made in 1 Peter 4:10–11. Here, gifts of both word and deed are mentioned. It is clear from 5:1–11 that the churches had 'overseers', or leaders, and the way in which these people exercised their ministry mattered, but the point is that particular spiritual gifts were not regarded as the exclusive preserve of certain leaders. This can be seen by comparing 1 Peter 4:11 with 5:1–3: in the former, the gifts are located in anyone, whereas in the latter, the advice given is specific to leaders. The caution to both members and leaders with gifts is that they should actively submit to Christ (5:6).

To return to Paul, in 1 Timothy 3:2 he connects the gift of teaching to church leadership, but it should not be imagined that only leaders taught. This gift was evidently exercised by a number of people (1 Corinthians 14:26). Also, Paul's understanding of his own leadership is further revealed in 1 Corinthians 5:1–5 and 12, where an issue of immorality is the focus of discipline. Once again, he does not call on the Corinthian church leaders to act, but for the church membership, together under Christ (v. 4), to resolve the issue corporately. Similarly, the implication is that if Paul were present, he would expect to make a leadership decision (v. 3) but would act collaboratively with the church and the Spirit in the matter (v. 4), not alone in a leadership role. Thus, the structure for dealing with this disciplinary matter does not depend on Paul's physical presence: the church deals with the issue corporately whether he is with them or not.

It is helpful to note again here (as mentioned in Chapter 9) that there is a difference between spiritual fruit and spiritual gifts. The growth of spiritual fruit (Galatians 5:22–26) connects with the process of 'sanctification', which expresses God's continuing work in Christian lives—taking, shaping and making more Christ-like (1 Thessalonians 5:23; Hebrews 2:10–11). The lists of spiritual gifts, however, connect with 'ministry' (the work or tasks of Christians), not personal sanctification. The fruit of the Spirit can be thought of as the 'spiritual DNA' of Christ applied to individual Christian lives. The gifts of the Spirit can be thought of as the 'ministerial DNA' of Christ applied to the church. Therefore, Paul expects any observer looking at Christians to see the image of Christ, and any individual who meets the church to meet the ministry of Christ (1 Corinthians 14:25). Thus, fruity Christians and a gifted church bear a certain 'family resemblance' to Christ, sharing the same relationship with God the Father (Romans 8:14–17). More than this, though, the church in its ministry resembles Christ. An example can be seen in Acts 3:1–10: if the names 'Peter and John' are replaced with the name 'Jesus', this incident becomes indistinguishable from a Gospel miracle. Peter and John have become recognizably 'like Christ' (ministerially, even if their personal spirituality is a work in process): the family likeness is evident.

To approach leadership and membership in a CM way, the difference between spiritual fruit and spiritual gifts has to be appreciated.

- The fruit that grows in Christian lives requires the time and attention of others if it is to be healthy. Therefore, 'orchard husbandry' is appropriate. Personal sanctification needs mutual assistance so that branches are pruned and fruit is nurtured. For fruit to grow properly, trees need individual attention.
- Spiritual gifts, by contrast, are to be used in the 'task' of ministry. Gifts are more like potatoes: the size and shape of each one is not particularly relevant. When God mashes them all together, then there's food for all. Neither do potato plants receive individual attention: the farmer pays attention to the soil. If the field is healthy, the crop will grow (this process is described in Chapter 15).

In a pyramidal structure, there is often the expectation that the top man will be both 'more sanctified', as it were, than church members, and will also be able to lead from the pinnacle in every area of ministry. This is because everyone in the pyramid takes their lead from the minister, so he should exhibit a wide variety of gifts, be more prayerful than anyone else and so on. In practice, this expectation tends to make it hard for the minister to submit his fruit (personal sanctification) to the scrutiny of others, and may limit the church to following his lead into only the areas of ministry for which he is gifted. When spiritual fruit and gifts are distinguished from each other, it allows ministers along with church members to seek personal attention (fellowship), which encourages the growth of spiritual fruit and enables everyone to grow in Christ. Also, recognizing that fruit and gifts are not necessarily connected releases ministers from the expectation that they will be gifted in every area of ministry—because their gifting, or lack of it, does not comment on their personal holiness. The CM minister will be gifted for church leadership, but this is a spiritual gift in its own right and not an amalgam of all other gifts. In a CM church, he will generally be able to encourage gifts in a wide variety of leaders, but specifically gifted to help create a structure in which the ministry and gifting of all can grow. In a pyramidal structure, the success of the church will probably depend on a gifted individual—the minister; in a CM church, success depends on how effectively the minister encourages members to collaborate with God and with one another.

One head

Paul describes Christ as the head of the body, and this can be considered in two different ways. First of all, Christ's headship can be understood in terms of marriage. In the same way that the first-century husband was the head of his family, so Christ is head of the church, his wife and bride to be (Ephesians 5:23–24). This image draws upon the custom of the time and religious Hebrew culture, whereby the husband looked to God (his Lord) and the wife looked to her husband (her Lord). Paul wrestled with this issue because he understood that God was no longer Lord of only the male head of each household, because Christ was Lord of all. On some occasions he affirmed the old covenant pattern (1 Corinthians 14:34–35), and on others the new (Galatians 3:26–28). In both instances, though, he used this image to underline the church's submission to Christ the head, looking to him for explanation and direction and trusting the church body to him.

Secondly, the headship of Christ can be thought of metaphorically. If the church is pictured as a human body, it is possible to ascribe different ministries to different parts—so perhaps teaching is the mouth, prophecy the eyes, charity the hands and so on. In this depiction of the body, Christ would be the mind. There are various passages that refer to the headship of Christ (Ephesians 4:15–16; Colossians 1:18; 2:17–19) but that kind of direct con-nection is not made, so perhaps it's best to put aside this particular interpretation. Headship is described in terms of authority or unity, and the points being made are these:

- All ministries are to be exercised for the good of others.
- All ministers come under the authority of Christ.
- Ministry, though diverse, is united because of Christ.

This connects with the expectation that every Christian will receive spiritual gifts and exercise them. Thus, in the church, all are ministers. The question is: how shall they collaborate appropriately? The New Testament answer seems to be that they work together under the headship of Christ, which is an intimate relationship because he is known through the Holy Spirit who grows fruit and gives gifts.

All one in Christ Jesus

Returning to Galatians 3:26–29, Paul indicates that the church is an egalitarian body. In his terms, 'there is neither Jew nor Greek, slave nor free, male nor female' because each person who 'belongs to Christ' is a 'son' of God and 'Abraham's seed'. This is a significant declaration: it flies in the face of first-century culture by ranking slaves and women with free men, and making everyone (including Gentiles) inheritors of Abraham. The point is that because the church belongs to Christ, and every individual Christian is a member of the same family and household, everyone, whatever their background, education or previous experience, receives the same attention from God. In terms of salvation, this means that there is only one reward (Matthew 20:1–16); in terms of ministry, it means that the Holy Spirit equips each person with gifts according to the direction of Christ.

In practice, this might mean that some leaders are younger than expected (1 Timothy 4:12), other leaders might have a highly dubious past (Acts 8:1–3; Galatians 1:13) and others again might let everyone down (Acts 15:37–38). It's worth asking a question: if the New Testament church had valued rank and skills above gifting and obedience, and if the choice of leaders had been left to a pyramidal leadership in Jerusalem (rather than to the Holy Spirit), how many of the apostles would have been leaders?

In our own day, CM not only allows but also encourages spiritual gifts, with the result that unexpected people occupy leadership roles. It is by no means uncommon in a CM church to find a well-educated person working under the leadership of someone who left school with no formal qualifications. Similarly, other leaders might be elderly or very young—people who, in pyramidal churches, would be regarded as those needing ministry. Training is still needed, as are safeguards, codes of good practice and working agreements—but they all facilitate the gifting that already exists and has been identified. Because CM recognizes the theology of the body of Christ, it allows that body to develop its various vital parts in accordance with the will of Christ. In other words, instead of looking for 'the right people' for jobs, CM works on the principle that Christ is sharing 'ministerial DNA' with various individuals—which will shape each of them for an appropriate task. This means that in a CM church, the 'obvious' people are not always the leaders, because Christ gifts whom he chooses for ministry.

Chapter 11

NEW COVENANT PEOPLE

To be under authority (in the biblical sense) is, in our society, countercultural. This chapter explores what it means to be a new covenant people who collaborate with the Holy Spirit under the authority of Christ. Links will be made with the biblical imagery used so far (holy priesthood, spiritual temple, household of faith, wife and body), recognizing that the whole covenant relationship between God and human beings obeys an 'unworldly economy': give to gain.

A covenant is an agreement between two parties. In the Old Testament, Abraham enjoyed a deep friendship with God, which was sealed by blood and sacrifice (Genesis 15), and there were similar friendships between God and other Old Testament characters. This friendship was continued and extended in the new covenant (John 15:15), sealed by the blood and sacrifice of Christ. The old covenant relationship can be summed up in the phrase 'I will be your God, and you will be my people' (Leviticus 26:12; Jeremiah 7:23; Ezekiel 37:27), and this too is continued in the new covenant. The new covenant, then, is a fulfilment of the old, and this understanding is most clearly stated in the book of Hebrews:

- The new covenant is superior to the old covenant (8:6–7).
- The new, like the old, is sealed with blood (12:24).
- The new, like the old, is a two-sided agreement, stating what God will do for his people and what his people must do for him (13:20–21).

The new covenant relationship is centred on the crucifixion and remembered in the Passover meal. In presiding over the Last Supper, Jesus declared that his blood, poured out for many, inaugurated the new covenant (Mark 14:22–25). The Passover meal therefore took on a new significance for the early church and became a regular focus for their worship and fellowship (1 Corinthians 11:23–26). If a new covenant theology remains with the cross, however, it will be incomplete. The resurrection of Christ, his ascension and Pentecost are also integral. The New Testament writers proclaim the vital nature of the cross because it is here that Christ offers his own life as the final, sufficient sacrifice for the sin of the world. The cross removes every impediment in the relationship between human beings and God. In this covenant, personal repentance is required. When sin is confessed and forgiven, however, there is nothing to keep the Spirit of God from the hearts and lives of human beings. He who is holy dwells with those who have confessed their unholiness. Those who put their trust in Christ are righteous after the pattern of their spiritual ancestor, Abraham (Romans 4:21–25), and, whatever their natural descent, they now occupy the same household.

THE NEW COVENANT IS DIFFERENT

In this new relationship, which is the fulfilment of the old covenant, just one thing has changed. The difference can be seen by making a study of the Holy Spirit in the Old Testament. Such a study could be a book in its own right, but briefly, in the old covenant, prophets (Ezekiel 2:2), kings (1 Samuel 10:6) and national figures (Judges 6:34) were filled with the Spirit of God. Occasionally, a person was filled with the Spirit as an exceptional event (2 Chronicles 15:1–7), but usually it was the national leaders who were equipped for 'ministry' in this way. It is also worth noting that the Spirit was both given (1 Samuel 10:9–10) and taken away (1 Samuel 16:14). These characters were the 'pinnacle people' of their day, exercising national ministries and equipped by the Spirit for the task, but they were under the authority of God. That is why the prophecy of Joel (2:28–29) is so extraordinary, because it speaks of everyone (including female servants!) receiving the same Spirit as King David or the prophet Elijah.

In the new covenant, all receive the Holy Spirit and all are 'friends of God' in the Old Testament sense (where friendship is a powerful bond, sealed by a blood-sacrifice). Once the friendship is made, each will come to the aid of the other, even fighting to the death on each other's behalf. In the new covenant, Jesus shed his blood for the sake of his friends (John 15:13), and through the sacrifice of Christ all may become the friends of God. James reminds Christians of the seriousness of this relationship when he cautions against treating the covenant lightly and urges them to be careful to repent when it is broken (James 4:4–9). From this understanding of covenant, the New Testament teaches that anyone who attacks a believer attacks Christ (Acts 9:4). Anyone who blesses a believer blesses Christ and anyone who ignores a believer ignores Christ (Matthew 25:40, 45). The friendship between God and an 'ordinary Christian' mirrors the friendship between God and Abraham, Solomon or Samuel. There is now no distinction between the high and the low because all are equally high.

A ONE-SIDED COVENANT?

In the contemporary church, we are sometimes guilty of preaching a one-sided covenant. If our individualistic culture is allowed to inform the church's view of covenant, we can end up sounding like a 'marketing drive' for God, telling only of what God will do for us and leaving out what we are to do for him. In the hope that people will find Christianity attractive, it can be all too easy to preach a 'benefit heavy' gospel. These are a few common examples:

- 'Come to me, all you who are weary and burdened, and I will give you rest' (Matthew 11:28). This is a wonderful verse, but what happened to the next words: 'Take my yoke upon you…' (v. 29)? Jesus is speaking, in fact, of a two-sided agreement, in which he promises rest if we will take on his yoke.
- 'Surely I am with you always, to the very end of the age' (Matthew 28:20b). Again, this is a wonderful verse, but where are verses 18–20, which speak of making disciples of all nations? The promise of Jesus' presence is clearly located in the context of evangelism. In this two-sided agreement, Jesus promises to be with us when we evangelize and live for him.
- 'All things work together for good' (Romans 8:28). The whole of this verse says that if we 'love the Lord' and are 'called according to his purpose', then whatever the circumstances, he will be working in them for good. This means something utterly different from 'all things work together for good'.
- 'We have an advocate with the Father, Jesus Christ the righteous; and he is the propitiation for our sins' (1 John 2:1, AV). The rest of this passage in 1 John 2 makes it clear that we are expected not to sin but to be living lives obedient to God's will, and tells us what we should do if we do sin.

The message of the new covenant is no different from the old. God still says, 'I will be your God, and you will be my people', and it is still a two-sided agreement:

- On God's side, Jesus seals the new covenant with his death and the Holy Spirit fills the new covenant people with life.
- On our side, we are the new priesthood and the new temple. Exemplary behaviour and obedience is expected of every priest, and each life, which is a living stone in the temple, is expected to be suitably holy (1 Corinthians 6:19–20).
- On both sides, there is sacrifice. Christ gives his life for us and we give our lives to him. He will be our God, and we will be his people.

NEW COVENANT PEOPLE

The new covenant, then, like the old covenant, is two-sided. To be God's people requires more than a ready acceptance of God's generosity; it requires that lives be lived sacrificially (Romans 12:1). This is the attitude that prompts Christians to be open to the Holy Spirit and to one another. Forgiveness is not to be hoarded, and neither is the self-giving of God or the gifts he gives. What is received must also, in turn, be given (Matthew 18:21–35). When we accept from God, we do so in covenant relationship, and intrinsic to the agreement is that we shall fulfil our side of it (Hebrews 13:20–21).

In the New Testament, Christians attempt to live sacrificially. It isn't easy, because the old life constantly pulls them, and on many occasions they fail: they are, like us, fallible human beings. Whether we look at the early church in Acts or through the epistles to the various churches addressed there, we see Christian people living sacrificially—appropriately for the new priesthood, which is also the new temple. Their part of the covenant is to keep themselves holy and to mediate the things of God to one another and to the world. In this, their view of one another is driven by their understanding of God. Much was expected of the old priesthood and much is expected of the new: priests of the new covenant must also cling to God, who is constantly doing a new thing among them.

There is an ancient proverb in the Near East that says, 'Blood is thicker than milk.' This means that a chosen friend (literally a 'blood-brother') is a closer relation than a birth-brother (who shared the same mother's milk). In the new covenant we see Christians living out a new proverb: 'Water is thicker than blood.' Those who are baptized in water regard their kinship with each other as stronger than their blood-ties. They live in a sacrificial relationship with one another because of their covenant relationship with God. What God gives them, they offer to others, and in this covenant all are equally sinful, equally forgiven, equally filled with the Spirit, and all, equally, are the new priesthood, temple, household, body and so forth. No one should regard their gifting as superior (2 Corinthians 10:17–18) or find pride in what is past (Philippians 3:1–11), because these are the things by which human beings set themselves up in leadership over others. In the new covenant, every living stone is vital to the integrity of the spiritual temple and every priest collaborates with both the Spirit and with the rest of the priesthood to live sacrificially for the benefit of others.

Encouragingly (for us), the New Testament church was not perfect. The Corinthian Christians neglected spiritual fruit and exercised spiritual gifts immaturely (and sinfully), like children wielding power tools. They also liked to be important, deciding a hierarchy among themselves (reminiscent of the disciples in Luke 9:46). The fact that Paul reasons with them in his letters shows his attitude to authority. Occasionally he ventures a personal opinion (1 Corinthians 7:12) or underlines common practice (11:16), but usually he does not direct their attention to himself, demanding their obedience; he directs their attention to Christ (7:10). He understands his task but does not confuse it with a role. He expects that the Spirit who leads him will be the same Spirit who leads them, and that the same Spirit will direct everyone. In our own day, those who regard the presence of the Holy Spirit as particular to the apostolic age (who believe, for example, that spiritual gifts were only given to the church for a brief time) will struggle with CM, because it is intrinsic to CM that the Spirit of Christ shares ministerial gifts for church leadership.

LEADERSHIP AND LORDSHIP

The heart of the matter is that our approach to leadership will depend on where we locate our theology. If it is located in the old covenant, we shall build a leadership pyramid. If it is shaped by contemporary culture, we shall probably interpret the New

Testament according to management techniques and, again, build a leadership pyramid. Only if we locate our thinking in New Testament theology, as understood by those who wrote it, shall we build CM.

Running like a thread through all of this is human nature. We are a fallen race and this has implications for the way in which we approach authority. Genesis 3 teaches that human beings don't like to be under the authority of anyone, particularly God. We prefer to reach our own conclusions and make our own decisions. As a result of the fall, we struggle in our relationships and wrestle with work, as we can see in Genesis 3:14–19. In this passage, of particular importance to the topic of leadership is verse 16: 'Your desire will be for your husband, and he will rule over you.' 'Rule' has the meaning of 'lording over' and specifically refers to the relationship between husband and wife.[1] The imagery of marriage, however, is also applied to the church (see Chapter 8) so it's worth taking account of the impact of this curse when considering leadership. Ministers who step into the position that Christ alone should occupy 'lord it over' the church, and the response of the members is to 'desire' this kind of leadership while at the same time finding it frustrating and demeaning. When this happens, it points to the fact that the theology of leadership is being located in a theology of the fall. At its most basic, all Christian leadership must point away from itself and towards Jesus Christ because he is the only Lord in the church and he is the Lord of all.

Pyramids lend themselves to lordship; CM does not. Centralism (as noted in Chapter 3), however appropriately shared, delegated or managed, is one short step from the kind of 'lording' leadership that Jesus says must not occur (Matthew 20:25–28). Far from being a bolt-on to existing structures, CM is revealed by the New Testament to be the most appropriate model for Christian leadership.

WHO SERVES WHOM?

Our individualistic society encourages people to regard themselves as free—masters of their own destiny—which makes the subject of redemption rather uncomfortable. To be 'redeemed' means to be 'bought back', and this was readily understood by first-century people because they were familiar with slavery. We, however, do not like to think of ourselves as owned: we prefer to think of ourselves as free. When it comes to religion, it is usual to think in terms of affiliation to a particular faith, to none or to several, but the Bible is of a different opinion. As Paul puts it, human beings have a choice about whom to serve (Romans 6:15–18), but no one is 'free'. No human being has the option of being masterless, so the choice concerns which master will be served. If we cannot accept that we have been 'bought at a price' (1 Corinthians 6:20) and are therefore 'owned' either by God or by another master, then we shall struggle to understand redemption, the new covenant, Jesus Christ, the church, or Christian leadership. The truth is that we have freedom only in inverse proportion to our submission—a pattern that reflects the nature of God and every aspect of incarnation.

Let's give ourselves a spiritual 'health check'. If God's promise is 'I will be your God and you will be my people', do we interpret this as a one-sided arrangement in which God will do everything for us (while our part of the covenant is graciously to allow him to do so)? To put it another way, do we belong to God or does he belong to us? Do we exist to serve God or does God exist to serve us?

To think further about this, let's compare what our attitude to prayer may be with that of New Testament Christians. Acts 4:1–31 is a helpful example. The apostles are arrested and threatened (vv. 3, 18, 21). When released, they pray with the church (v. 24). The content of their prayer is to ask God to strengthen them in spite of the threats. In diagrammatic form, their attitude is this:

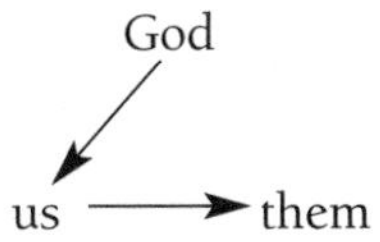

The apostles ask God to give them the strength they need to continue to speak. They do not ask God to change their persecutors or to change the circumstances. They ask God to change them, because they are in a covenant relationship with him and they want to serve God appropriately. They recognize that they may end up in jail (or worse) and they do not expect an easy time. They do not even ask God to speak to the members of the Council (v. 23) in a 'spiritual way'. They have a clear understanding of what they must do, and simply ask God to fill them with boldness (v. 29).

Now let's compare their attitude with a prevalent attitude today. Let's think of a difficult situation that we face. Perhaps our church buildings are being vandalized or maybe we are the target of anti-social behaviour. What do we pray: that God will change the hearts of the vandals? That God will intervene on our behalf and make the nasty people go away (while we stay indoors under the duvet)? In diagrammatic form, that attitude is like this:

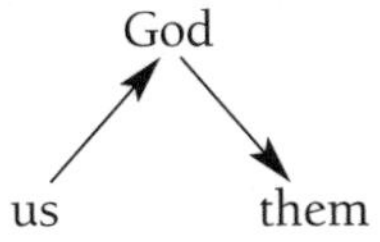

In effect, we ask God to change others without doing anything ourselves. When this attitude is present, it shows a misunderstanding about what a covenant relationship means: in effect, we are treating God as our servant. The expectation is that God will change circumstances and people so that our lives become simpler and more comfortable.

In the New Testament church, God does intervene directly on occasion (Acts 5:17–21). The church does not ask for these interventions, though; they are as surprising to the Christians as to everyone else (12:5–16). The disciples' attitude was to ask God to change them so that they could live as God wanted—aware that this would make their lives more complicated and uncomfortable. Acts records that God answered their prayers and demonstrated his presence, and that the church continued to grow.

In order to compare their attitudes with ours, let's ask the questions again: in what terms do we think of the new covenant? Do we exist to serve God or does he exist to serve us? Do we ask God to give us strength and boldness for the task (along with the gifts to achieve it) or do we ask God to sort out the problems directly so that we don't have to? Do we ask God to take the hits on our behalf, or do we expect to receive blows for him (Matthew 5:39)? Is it possible that some of our unanswered prayers and lack of church growth are connected to our misunderstanding of covenant?

New Testament Christians had a clear understanding of what it meant to be the household of faith—redeemed, new covenant people. They were keenly aware of all the cost to Christ and the blessings that the Spirit shared with them. In their obedience and service, they patterned themselves after Jesus, and the covenant 'met in the middle'. When we misunderstand the covenant (thinking it means that God is our servant), it's a short step to misunderstanding leadership. If God exists to serve us, then it must be the job of his representatives (the ministers) to do this too. Therefore, if we face problems, we tell the minister and expect him to sort them out on our behalf. Both traditional pyramidal leadership and servant leadership tend to promulgate this view.

WHAT IS THE CHURCH FOR?

Examining any aspect of early church life reveals the same values expressed in both community and collaboration. Prayer is mostly corporate, and action is collaborative (with God and with each other). Every aspect of Christian life was underpinned with the axiom 'give to gain'. That was the early Christians' understanding of God's action and also of their service to him. In our culture, a fundamental value is 'trade to gain', but when this attitude is allowed to permeate the church we are left with a transactional faith:

- Members pay leaders to make the church successful.
- Prayer becomes a process of bargaining.
- Worship must be entertaining.
- Teaching must be exciting.
- Pastoral care is seen as a 'service contract'.
- Evangelism becomes marketing.

These attitudes arise out of our individualistic culture, in which commitment to an organization depends on an acceptable 'return' (trade to gain). When members face problems, the expectation is of immediate personal attention; for the rest of the time, association (in a non-costly personal way) with a successful organization is sufficient. In the church, if transaction replaces sacrificial partnership, the old life is retained and, instead of new life replacing it, a contemporary approximation is added. The body of Christ then tends not to exhibit the marks of death and resurrection, but of plastic surgery!

According to the Bible (as we have seen already), the church exists for two reasons: to go out and to build up. In both aspects of church life, individuals live their faith by the presence of spiritual fruit and exercise ministry through spiritual gifts. God redeems his people so that they might be with him, proclaim the good news and fight against evil. Therefore, every fruit and gift is given for the benefit of others. God by his Spirit works 'in' the church to work 'through' the church, and this pattern is true both for the individual and the corporate body. It is a holy priesthood, a spiritual temple, a household and a body. The primary relationship for every Christian is with God; the secondary relationship for every Christian is with each other. Church is a community of faith.

Collaborative Ministry is a way of organizing the church in partnership with God and each other. It provides a suitable environment for both 'building up' and 'going out' activities. CM holds together the sanctification of the individual, personal humility and the exercise of gifted ministry.

THE NEW COVENANT WAY

Wherever we look in the Bible, we read the same lesson. We could continue by studying the imagery of shepherd and sheep, the army of God (which, in our present internationally uncertain world, has difficult militaristic overtones), king and kingdom and so forth, but the message would be identical. Christ is the one great shepherd, the commanding officer, the king; we are the sheep, the legionaries, the holy nation. Christ is our master and the church should accept no substitute. In the church, all Christians are shoulder to shoulder and, although ministerial tasks may differ, everyone shares the same 'rank'. Every image underlines the level ground upon which individual Christians stand: they are never used to indicate a hierarchy of leadership.

Collaborative Ministry rests on a practical theology which declares that Jesus is Lord, and the church a gathering of his disciples. The church belongs to God; it is his possession, and he chooses to breathe his Spirit upon it, growing spiritual fruit in individual lives and giving spiritual gifts for ministry. Gifts may vary but each Christian, whatever their task, is an ordinary person who is called and equipped by God. A fundamental value of CM is that each ordinary person serves God, the church and the world, extraordinarily.

The old covenant describes what will and must be done to make possible the promise 'I will be your God and you will be my people'. The new covenant is the living embodiment of the same promise—in Christ and, because of the Holy Spirit, in the body of Christ. CM is an attempt to respond to the Spirit, obey Jesus Christ and minister to the world as a new covenant people in a new covenant way.

NOTE

1 This is considered in detail in Chapter 5 of *Marriage—Restoring Our Vision*.

Part Three

BUILDING A COLLABORATIVE MINISTRY STRUCTURE

Chapter 12

DEVELOPING COLLABORATIVE MINISTRY

Part Three looks at the practicalities of building Collaborative Ministry in the contemporary church. It offers practical suggestions for beginning the process of CM, addresses issues, gives advance warning of problems and challenges, and outlines the benefits and possibilities. Although CM can be implemented in small or large churches, within one area of ministry or across a multiplicity of congregations, for the sake of simplicity Part Three describes the development of CM within a single church. The practical outworking of CM can then be applied appropriately to any situation.

By this point, we should have two clear understandings:

- The pros and cons of traditional pyramidal leadership.
- A theology for collaborating with God and each other, which defines CM.

When it comes to detail, every church will be different, but, to use the image of buildings, pyramidal leadership might be thought of as a stately home and CM as a bungalow. All stately homes are different, but there are enough similarities to recognize the genre. To exist, they require both personnel and a hierarchy. They are so costly to run that, these days, few remain in private hands and the majority survive only by diversifying into tourism. Similarly, bungalows come in all shapes and sizes, but all are recognizable as bungalows. One can be compact, another large; the difference is in how far they spread out. In Britain, bungalows tend to carry no kudos, so the size of bungalow will usually reflect the number of occupants. CM is like a bungalow in that it is defined by the number of collaborators. A small congregation can structure for CM as can a large congregation. All that is required is that suitable foundations are laid underneath (in this case, a sound theology of leadership, membership and the relationship between the two).

BEGINNING TO BUILD

Building a CM structure affects everyone in the church, and this means that the whole church must in some way engage in the process of establishing CM. This introduces a conundrum: if a church operates traditionally (under the authority of the minister and 'central leaders'), the whole church is not organized in such a way as to make this kind of decision. The most likely effect of this is that if a church wants to engage in CM, it will probably look at the minister and say, 'Minister, this CM sounds really good. Will you implement it, please?' There is a certain irony here, which points towards a contradiction: for a church to pursue CM, the minister will probably need to take a principal role in the process!

Strong leadership

Paradoxically, to lead a church collaboratively, the minister has to be strong. For example, he needs to be able to allow others to take real responsibility—which may lead to success or failure. He must keep his hands off even when he knows he could do a better (and quicker) job. He needs the spiritual wit to recognize his own ministry and the ministry of others, and the personal strength to reject pressure. He must have a strong sense of self, because if he finds personal comfort in busyness, a full diary or being the central person (needed, gifted and important), then he is going to have problems with CM. The minister must be strong enough to rejoice when others succeed and get the credit: one of the costs of CM to the minister is that he is unlikely to build a personal reputation. So CM demands strength, but of a different kind from the pyramidal minister's, where a firm hold of the reins is required and decisions, vision and leadership all come from the top. The CM minister has to insist that others are respected, listened to, enabled, resourced and followed.

Let's look at the same issue from another angle. The minister is central to the process of CM because the church cannot operate CM without his leadership. Thus the paradox is unevenly weighted: a minister can decide to build CM in his church, but a church cannot begin CM without the commitment of the minister. The reason for this is the centralist starting place: if the minister is the pinnacle leader, then part of the process of beginning CM involves his willing agreement to climb down and acknowledge that the church does not belong to him but to Christ. Once CM is established, then the church can perpetuate it regardless of the minister. This tends to unsettle 'overseers', with the effect that at some point they will probably say, 'Minister, the CM in your church is really good—but who's going to replace you? What will we do if you leave?' This highlights the fact that CM cannot be easily bolted on to existing structures. So, if we believe that CM is a suitable expression of New Testament theology, where do we start?

A threefold initiative

To get CM under way, the following will need to be addressed:

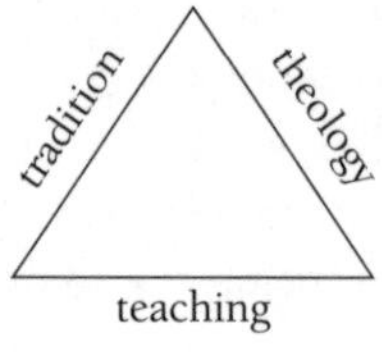

This can be thought of as a transitional pyramid to replace the old one, but this shape has no 'right way up' and no one occupies the pinnacle. What the shape shows is that these three aspects are all equally important. Let's look at each one:

- Tradition means 'the way we do things now'. The whole church needs to understand its historical and present leadership structure. We can work out our tradition by using Part One of this book.
- Theology means 'the way we understand the Bible'. The whole church needs a good grasp of what it means to be church in a New Testament, collaborative way. Basically, that's Part Two of this book.
- Teaching means 'be like me'. This is the practice of CM as implemented and exhibited by the church: Part Three of this book.

Experience suggests that it is not possible to address these three aspects independently. There is no prescribed order, but over an initial period all three must be addressed. Therefore, an examination of structures will probably parallel programmes that outline the theology, while, at the same time, opportunities are found to model CM.

A timetable

The timetable will vary, depending on the local culture. Some churches deal with change quickly; others take longer. As a general rule, though, the timetable for CM will probably look like this:

- Six–twelve months to assess the tradition, begin the theology and come to a point of decision.
- Three years of initial implementation to first review.

- Two years of further implementation to second review.
- Five years to the next review (ad infinitum).

Because CM concerns the whole church, it takes time. In some churches it will be right to begin with the theology, follow up with a review of structures and then introduce CM ideas. In other churches, it may be right to begin with a review of structures, which leads into an introduction of CM ideas, while the focus on theology is going on in the background. Conceivably, some churches will be ready to implement CM straight away, but experience suggests that it will be a few keen leaders who want to implement immediately, not the whole church. If pyramidal leadership were being continued, this would be fine, but if CM is to be built, the keen must wait for the reluctant! At the very least, it's helpful to ensure that the theology is in place and that everyone has a clear understanding of traditional structures; otherwise, a minority impose the decision on the majority before they are ready to make it. If CM is rushed into without a proper consultation, the result may resemble the exodus —even if the pinnacle leaders have made the right decision, the people will probably moan for 40 years.

The first six–twelve months are vital. It is here (teaching by example) that pinnacle leaders begin to demonstrate (by action) the truth of the theology. It is here that collaboration begins. Building a CM structure is not an overnight affair. We begin where we are and move towards a new structure. In this process, the early stages will inevitably be 'pyramidal', so the existing leadership will be first to grapple with the change.

A WORKSHOP

When the church is ready, it's time to run a workshop. This could be done all in one day or over a period of time (perhaps spread over three evenings). Depending on the church, it could be done with a gathering of leaders, perhaps on an 'away day', or as part of a whole church weekend away. The workshop could be done with home group leaders and then they could do the same exercise with their home groups, or groups could be brought together for a central meeting.

So welcome to a practical introduction to CM! As we have already said, CM does not provide a blueprint, so every church will need to pursue it in a manner appropriate to its own situation. How and with whom a church chooses to run the workshop is up to that church, but let's look at the content:

- Session 1: an examination of traditional structures with reference to some theology.
- Session 2: an examination of the current leadership structure.
- Session 3: a broad-brush CM beginning.

Each session will take about one hour, so with prayer, worship, lunch, questions, buzz groups, feedback, lunch and fisticuffs, this is a whole day's programme.

Session 1

Begin this session by presenting the various models of pyramidal leadership. The diagrams in Part One may be reproduced for this purpose. In the presentation, offer as much or as little theology as is appropriate to the occasion, but as an absolute minimum it will be helpful to refer to priesthood and the temple. It is critical, though, to allow enough time for each model of leadership to be properly discussed. It is particularly helpful if people make connections between the diagrams and their own experience.

If the first diagram (the traditional pyramid) is met with the response 'Seen it, done it, got the T-shirt', don't worry. By the time the servant leadership diagrams are the focus of attention, those kind of comments will probably have been replaced by a growing concentration and (we hope) excitement.

Session 2

You will need a large sheet of paper, a couple of red and green marker pens, plus enough blue pens for everyone. For this session, people sit in a circle around the sheet of paper (if necessary, tape several sheets together to make a large piece).

Invite people to suggest the various groups, activities, events and ministries that make up 'our church'. As each one is identified, ask them to write it on the sheet of paper (in blue), in letters big enough for everyone to see. Include all administrative, spiritual, pastoral and maintenance activities, and don't forget annual events.

For the next stage, one or two people can wield the red and green pens. Ask two questions, in turn, of every blue note on the paper:

- If this group, activity, event or ministry wants to do something, whom does it ask? Draw in green the 'positive line of authority' to whomever, or whatever, will give permission.
- If this group, activity, event or ministry is doing something wrong, who will tell it to stop? Draw in red the 'negative line of authority' to whomever, or whatever, will issue the reprimand.

When the exercise is complete, discuss it. Are most of the green and red lines going to the same person? Is that person the minister? If the lines go to a group of people, is the minister the chair of that group (in other words, in reality, do those lines go to the minister too)? In any church where the lines converge on one person or one group, this demonstrates pyramidal leadership—and who is in charge.

Look out also for anomalies:

- Are there leaders to whom no red or green lines connect? If so, what exactly are they supposed to be leading? They have a title but no authority.
- Are there groups, activities or events with no green or red lines? If so, why are they not under any kind of authority?
- Are there any groups, activities, events or leaders that have green and red lines going to two different people or groups? Is this sensible?

In a pyramidal structure, these independent satellites and anomalies always occur. They may be benign (no one has noticed) or malignant (a deliberate power base) but they will be there. It may be right to dwell briefly on these inconsistencies, just to recognize that they exist and need attention.

Now for the final part of Session 2. Looking at what the group has drawn, it's time to ask four questions:

- Is this structure sustainable? Particularly where the minister is overloaded with green and red lines; is it humanly possible for him to sustain this workload?
- How does a new person get into the church? Is it easy or very complex?
- Is the church organized for growth? If the church grew to ten times its current size, would the pattern of leadership have to change? Looking at the same issue from the opposite direction, is the present leadership structure prohibiting growth?
- In what ways, if any, does this resemble a New Testament Christian church?

It may be useful briefly to revisit the leadership models used in Session 1. What kind of leadership structure does the sheet of paper describe? If the church is happy with its 'traditional' way of being church, why? If not, why not?

Session 3

You will need enough paper and pencils for everyone. Split people into buzz-groups (ideally, between three and six people per group). They will need to have sight of the large sheet of paper from Session 2, so this can be either left on the floor or stuck to a wall.

The object of this exercise is to work out which groups, activities, events and people are obviously working in the same area of ministry. Ask each buzz-group to think about what's on the large sheet, and start to organize them together into 'categories'. For example, there may be various groups for children, or adults, which are all working in the same area of ministry—like this:

- Sunday school, after-school club, youth fellowship, toddlers, nursery.
- Home groups, prayer groups, Alpha group.

A large church might identify six, ten or more categories of ministry; a small church may identify three or four. When the buzz-groups are finished (or struggling), come back together in a plenary session. On a fresh sheet of paper, agree some of the 'categories' through input from the various buzz-groups, and try to note some kind of descriptive title for each. At this stage, some of the groups, activities, events and people noted on the large sheet of paper will not fit readily into any category of ministry. Don't worry about this for the moment; concentrate instead on the obvious clusters. At the end of the feedback session, there will probably be a number of categories of ministry and some fragments of ministry that don't seem to fit anywhere. Now it's time to ask two final questions. Taking each new category in turn, ask:

- Do the leaders of the constituent groups, activities and events in each category meet, pray and plan together?
- Should they?

The next step is to suggest that each category of ministry has a 'Leadership Team'. This team would be constituted of one leader, or representative, from each of the current constituent groups. Therefore, in the examples above, the 'children's nurture team' might have five members (if one person represents Sunday school, another the after-school club and so on) and the 'adult nurture team' might have nine (if there are six home groups, two prayer groups and one Alpha course). The task of each of these two teams would be to meet, pray together and plan their area of ministry in a way that enables the currently independent work to join forces (collaborate). This is the first broad-brush consideration of CM. Instead of the groups, activities, events and their leaders tracing their authority (their green and red lines) to the pinnacle of the pyramid, it is being suggested that together they *are* a pinnacle.

If, as a result of Session 2, we are looking at a piece of paper with three ministry categories on it, then we are looking at a three-pinnacle structure. If there are 27 categories on the paper, then we are looking at 27 pinnacles. The theology tells us that Jesus Christ will be Lord of each one; in practical terms, we shall now need to think about how these categories of ministry can function collaboratively with both freedom and accountability. Also, it will need to be established how the various areas of ministry can collaborate together across a whole church structure.

MOVING ON

The workshop now needs grounding. At this early stage, the beginnings of CM might be mistaken for sensible delegation. This is because, as a first step, what is being established is Collaborative Leadership (CL). Don't worry about this: the theology is going on in the background, and the penny will drop as the Spirit speaks to hearts. If the structure looks like delegated CL now, it soon won't.

Is there a consensus to proceed with CM? If there is (and if a church has got this far, in all likelihood there will be), then a working group must be established. The object of this group will be:

- To put together 'job descriptions' for the individual Leadership Teams. These descriptions will specify expectations within each area of ministry.
- To work out how the various teams relate to one another. This locates each area of ministry within a whole-church structure.
- To work out where the ministries that don't easily fit into any team cluster fit into the whole church structure. This can be done by making them a 'sub-team' (not part of, but under the authority of, one of the new teams). Alternatively, they can be connected to an individual minister or to an existing central decision-making body, such as a church council.

This process will take time, and should not be undertaken without the knowledge and input of the groups, activities, events and people concerned. In all probability, the job descriptions will take several months of discussion, modification and revision. We have, however, begun.

Chapter 13

GETTING DOWN TO DETAIL

Working out the details for Collaborative Ministry will take time, effort and—if a large number of church members take part in the process, as they should—what will feel like a certain amount of repetitive discussion. To keep this in perspective, it is helpful to remember that pyramidal leadership evolved over centuries, so spending a few months developing CM is, by comparison, light speed! As we get down to the details, the aim is to encourage collaboration throughout the church—within each group, activity, event and individual ministry and across each category of ministry. This moves CL into CM and underlines the fact that communication is essential.

In order to establish Leadership Teams, it will be necessary to address their constitution, brief, scope and accountability. It's useful to consider a practical example so, for the purposes of this book, the adult nurture team mentioned in Chapter 12 will be used. Let's look at the four aspects in turn.

CONSTITUTION

The constitution describes who is on a particular team. In the case of our adult nurture team, there are nine automatic members: the six home group leaders, the two prayer group leaders and the Alpha course leader. On reflection, it may be discovered that the church has other adult groups that should be represented on this team. There would then be additional constituent members but, for the sake of this example, let's stick to nine. In order for the team to function, it will need a team leader. This could be someone already on the team (any of the nine) or someone co-opted for the purpose. The role of team leader is that of facilitator: they make sure that meetings happen, that every constituent group is represented and that the brief, scope and accountability are adhered to.

Let's ask a question: what if one of the home group leaders can't make the team meeting? It doesn't matter, as long as someone else from that home group attends. CM is not person-dependent: if a group leader is ill or on holiday, someone else can represent that group. In terms of workload, it may be appropriate for the team representative to be someone other than the group leader anyway. CM is not about role but task; it's not a hierarchy but a collaboration, and a group member is just as qualified to express the group's intentions as the group leader is.

So far, though, all that has been done is to gather these people for an extra meeting. None of the green or red lines identified in Session 2 of the workshop has been cut and neither has the team been given anything to do. That's why they need a brief.

BRIEF

The brief describes the work that the team will do and the responsibilities they accept. For example, we may decide that the adult nurture team should propose or create the teaching programme for home groups. They might do this by deciding to follow a published course, they might decide that each home group should follow a different programme, or they may decide to ask the minister or someone else to prepare a specific series for study. Ultimately, however, the team members will sound out members of the groups they represent, discuss their input in the team meeting and make a decision. The team may also be given the task of identifying and appointing constituent group leaders. This will then make the team responsible for who leads a home group, a prayer group or an Alpha course.

Some green and red lines of authority have now been redirected to the team. If a home group leader wants to do something, they ask the team. If a home group leader is doing something that they shouldn't, it's the team that tells them to stop; and, at rock bottom, the team hires or fires the leaders. The team might also initiate new groups and evangelistic opportunities. Therefore, red and green lines now connect constituent groups to the team: the team has authority.

Common to all teams, it should provide support for leaders. If its constituent members are all group leaders, then this can be done in team meetings. If team members are group representatives rather than leaders, then another support mechanism will be needed for group leaders—and the provision of this can be a team task. Every team, as part of its brief, should encourage and identify the exercise of gifts in the development of its ministry. In other words, members of the team are always on the lookout for others who exhibit gifts that can be developed, and keep a supportive eye on those who are exercising them.

The team will also need to establish a pattern for meeting. Some teams will benefit from meeting on a monthly or six-weekly basis. For other teams, it will be more appropriate to meet on a termly or even biannual basis. The frequency of meeting will be, in large part, driven by the brief.

SCOPE

One of the key factors in CM is money. In a pyramidal structure, finances tend to be collected assiduously and released reluctantly. In CM, the rationale is different. Money is given to the church to fund ministry, so the money is given to the ministers. In terms of the adult nurture team, their brief makes them responsible for this area of ministry, so how much money will they need to make it happen? They may want to buy resources, bring in outside speakers or fund events. It is not part of CM thinking that this team should repeatedly approach a central decision-making body with funding requests, because the team is responsible for its own decisions. Unless the team is funded, the church runs the risk of discussing the same issue all over again in a different decision-making body, and possibly overturning decisions that have already been taken. Therefore, the team needs a budget.

The budget for each team will be determined by the cost of fulfilling its brief. A team may require £100, £1000 or £10,000 a year to do its job, but the rule of thumb is this: for as long as the team remains within budget, how it chooses to spend the money is up to the team. At this point, it should be remembered that the team is expected to work with other teams (not in competition with them) and under the authority of Christ. They are spending his money, not church money.

This introduces a second key aspect of CM: boundaries. It is wise to define the scope of the team in terms that allow complete freedom within a defined, overall pattern, but demand reference if the team wishes to implement something outside that defined, overall pattern. In this example of an adult nurture team, establishing additional home groups and prayer groups might fall within the defined, overall pattern, as would (within budget) providing groups with study material from the Old Testament, the New Testament or more general Christian spirituality. The team therefore fulfils its brief by making such decisions on a regular basis. If the team decides to terminate all groups, or demands that they all meet at 2 o'clock in the morning, or wants to spend three million euros on a community hot-tub experience, or insists that home groups study an ant farm while gargling with yoghurt, this would probably (!) fall outside the defined, overall pattern. These decisions could then only be implemented after reference and agreement from another decision-making body within the church (accountability). Therefore, although the team may exercise significant ministry within its boundaries, it may not change those boundaries itself.

By identifying a budget and boundaries, the team's authority is limited. The brief and scope may give the team a very broad remit, but there are boundaries. If the team wishes to make decisions beyond its scope or brief, then it must refer elsewhere.

ACCOUNTABILITY

Accountability establishes the green and red lines that run to the teams, and describes where they fit into the overall church structure. In other words, if a team needs permission to do something beyond its brief or scope, whom does it ask? Similarly, if there is a problem with a team, who will sort things out? Accountability is the practical application of teams being under authority.

If the structure were a delegated pyramid, these green and red lines of accountability would probably run from the teams to the minister. In most CM churches, however, it will probably be sensible to create a 'team leaders' team' and connect the lines of authority to this. In that way, the collaborative pattern is continued. In the same way that each team enables its constituent groups to collaborate in ministry together, the team leaders' team enables the constituent teams to collaborate in the overall ministry of the church. This team will also have a constitution, brief, scope, accountability, a team leader and so forth. Primarily, its task will be threefold:

- To be a place of information and communication. In other words, team leaders tell one another what's happening in their area of ministry, outline future plans, agree to join forces for particular events and projects, share concerns, receive mutual support and so forth.

- Within the brief and scope of team leaders, decisions can be made about the constituent teams. Thus the red and green lines that run from team leaders to the teams (the extent of the team leaders' team's authority) are defined.
- Matters beyond the brief or scope of team leaders are referred elsewhere. This is where the red and green lines that run to the team leaders' team are defined—that is, under whose authority it comes. In a delegated pyramid, this would (finally) be the minister. In most CM churches, it will probably be to the established church council or equivalent body.

As an example, let's say that the adult nurture team wants to promote a course of study which is very expensive. The team does not have the budget for the course, so it first refers the matter to team leaders. Possibly, one or two of the other teams are working below budget, so they may say, 'Well, look, this sounds good, so we'll release a quarter of our budget to you, and with the pooled funds you can organize it.' If the team leaders' team agrees, then the adult nurture team has its extra finance and can go ahead. If, on the other hand, the other team leaders are dubious about the worthiness of the proposed course, they may say 'No' and the matter ends there. If the team leaders think the course is a good idea but cannot fund it, then the matter will be referred to the church council for a final decision (and, if this is positive, for a release of additional funds).

In this structure, each team is accountable to team leaders for decisions and dependent on team leaders for information. It is recommended that each team:

- At a designated time of year, reports verbally to the church council.
- Before the end of the financial year, submits a budget request for the following year.
- Prepares a written report for the annual meeting of the whole church.

AN OVERVIEW

At this point, it's worth briefly standing back to regard the structure as a whole. The CM church no longer resembles a pyramid because the roles of both the minister and the original central decision-making body have changed. These changes are considered in detail in Chapters 14 and 15, but for now let's recognize two fundamental shifts.

First of all, a significant proportion of the ministerial task that was previously the province of the minister and the church council is now being done by the teams and their constituent groups. Ministry has become collaborative, reflecting the theology of a priesthood of all believers.

Second, the vast majority of red and green lines identified in Session 2 of the workshop are now attached to groups of people, the teams and the church council—not to individuals and, specifically, not to the minister. He, just like every other leader or member, has become part of the structure. He is still the minister, but he now exercises his leadership from within the church, not from the top of it. The exercise of authority has become collaborative, reflecting the theology that Jesus Christ is in charge.

LENGTH OF SERVICE

Getting back to the details, it's useful to define every aspect of the commitment expected of leaders, which includes the 'length of tenure'. Every church will decide which 'jobs' this applies to and will come up with a different answer, but it is recommended that in a CM church the period of tenure for team leaders (at least) should be defined. Experience shows that a three-year commitment is best, on the basis of one year in the first instance, and then for a further two years if the appointment is working well. There are two reasons for limiting the length of leadership:

- For the sake of the leader.
- For the sake of the church.

Leaving someone to do the same job for 40 years tends to be detrimental both to the leader and to the church. Long service confuses task with role, directs the life of the leader in only one direction (when perhaps they could flourish in several) and excludes others from exercising their own gifting. Long service also tends to be counterproductive in the life of the church because individuals can make themselves so indispensable that the whole body is forced to dance to their personal tune. In CM, the focus is on individual development, even if the organization must change accordingly. Therefore, a built-in 'step down' date is to be recommended in every area of ministry.

The benefit to the church is that after ten years of CM, every leadership role will have been filled by at least three different people. Thus, understanding of each ministry is disseminated throughout the church community. In all honesty, however, this is an aspect of CM that causes even the most committed to wobble: the thought of finding yet another treasurer can challenge anyone's theology of gifting. But experience shows that the Spirit prompts the right person at the right time.

WORKING WITHIN DENOMINATIONAL STRUCTURES

Although developing CM within an existing denominational structure may take some lateral thinking, it can be not only possible but positive. Some churches may have no option but to organize their leadership structure within specific guidelines, and others (for example, the Church of England) must accord with the law of the land as well as the law of the church. Therefore, many individual churches are not free simply to change, at will, either their existing leadership structure or their church officers. What is at issue in CM, however, is not what is done but how it is done. If we focus on a Church of England minister as an example, when he is appointed he vows to pastor the people entrusted to his care, which will include thousands of people living in that area. The question is: does he fulfil his vow when he personally cares for each person or when he organizes a team of people to minister pastorally? The issue is not about what is done, but about how it is done.

CM interprets leadership in terms of task, not role. Therefore, the minister does not lead through his personal role; he leads by enabling others to lead, and the task is shared under the authority of Christ. Different denominations and churches will decide which aspects of ministry must remain with the minister. The CM church remains under the authority of its overseers; CM is not a unilateral declaration of independence. Many tasks that have traditionally been attached to the minister's role, however (akin to the pastoral example above), are likely to fall into the category of ministry that can be shared. Neither the practice of CM nor its theology removes the need for a minister (or for ordination, commissioning, appointment, or whatever a church or denomination does to mark out particular people for ministerial leadership); what it does is to enable ministers and members to share ministry together in the radical fashion of New Testament Christians.

At first glance, teams can be mistaken for new sub-committees (delegation). When their brief and scope are considered, however, it becomes clear that they are autonomous units linked only by communication and final authority to the existing church council. The minister may be involved with some teams and not with others, but the shared task is undertaken by all. The existing decision-making body may or may not be replaced by the team leaders' team, but the two can work happily in conjunction, particularly if each member of the central body is a representative on a team. In the adult nurture team example, this would mean that the nine people already on the team would be joined by an additional representative (from the church council), increasing the total to ten. The role of this new representative would be to keep the team abreast of what's going on in the church council, and vice versa. Thus each team can be informed by their team leader (through the team leaders' team) and by their church council representative.

Organizing the structure in this way has three positive benefits.

- Because communication is vital, the more connections there are with other teams and decision-making bodies, the better.
- It means that everyone in the church (council members included) is engaged in the task of ministry: there are no passengers.
- It defines the size of the central decision-making body, which will probably need to change once the teams are in place.

SOME QUESTIONS

Getting to grips with the details will raise a few issues:

- What should the 'teams' be called?
- Is it advisable to set up one team at a time or every team at the same time?
- Is this a version of cell church?

Calling the ministry categories 'teams' imposes certain connotations, particularly as the concept of 'teamworking' is increasingly popular in secular management. If they are called 'groups', though, there are overtones of fellowship. If they are 'committees', there are overtones of pyramidal authority. If they are 'work groups' then there are overtones of temporary exploration—and so on and so forth. On balance, the word 'team' seems to work because it carries overtones of 'doing this together'. In the end, it doesn't matter what they are called as long as they are structured appropriately, but for the sake of continuity they will continue to be referred to in this book as teams.

It will also be necessary to decide on a method of implementation. One way to do this is by evolving into CM one team at a time, perhaps taking three months to establish each team before moving on to the next. Alternatively, all teams can be established at once. There are pros and cons with each approach. In the first approach, each team is seen to be working properly before continuing with the process. The downside is that, for a while, two contradictory systems are being operated at once (the original pyramid and CM)—a process that invites each system to trip up the other. Also, if any team fails to take off, it's possible to spend far too long with it while ignoring the next team, which might take off very quickly. If a complete team structure is implemented at once, this has the advantage of replacing one structure with another, but can feel very risky to everyone involved. Ultimately, each church will need to decide on how to proceed—from the shallows or straight into the depths—one team at a time, or all at once.

Is CM another version of cell church? No, because CM is task-based. It looks similar to cell church at first glance because it structures ministry by grouping disciples around Jesus. A second look at the leadership structure shows the difference: the organization of cell church is pyramidal, but the organization of CM is not. CM defines and divides both ministry and authority across the whole church rather than building layers. At some point, however, the CM church will need to address the issue of fellowship. It is quite possible to extend any team's brief to include Bible study, prayer, fellowship and so forth—and then teams may appear to be cells even though they are not.

If the team's brief is expanded in this way, then the team replaces home groups for the team members. Their team functions most of the time as a home group, but every third, fourth or sixth meeting it functions according to its team brief. This only works if members are disciplined and do not allow team business to bleed into every home group meeting. Also, the team will need a group leader when it is functioning as a home group (who may be the team leader or someone else in the team). For the children's nurture team that we pictured in Chapter 12, or for other teams, this might make a lot of sense but, for the adult nurture team of our example, life would become rather complex. If this team operates as a regular home group in its own right, because each team member is already the leader of their own home group, this would double their load. They would be the leader of their own group, but also a member of the 'team group'. On the other hand, it's just as workable to separate teams from home groups and for team members to belong to both—giving out in one area of ministry and receiving in the other. This does, however, highlight the extra time commitment required of team members (more about this in Chapter 15). In the end, whether team functions are combined with fellowship functions or separated, in either incarnation team members will experience camaraderie as a by-product of working together.

THE CM STRUCTURE

So far, the CM process has focused only on existing events, groups and ministries. This is because starting 'where we are' is fundamental to the nature of CM, as compared to leadership structures based on 'where we want to be' (if only we had sufficient leaders). It has already been noted that CM is a one-size-fits-all approach to ministry, so what does this mean in practice? If the first step into CM involves establishing teams of existing leaders, what happens to the structure when the church grows or new ministry begins?

To think about numerical growth in church membership first, what happens if a church of 100 members increases fivefold? Perhaps, when CM began, there were seven teams: these might be the adult nurture and children's nurture teams already mentioned, two service-planning teams (one for each congregation), a buildings team (for maintenance and development), a finance team and a pastoral team. The fact that the church now has 500 members will probably make little difference to the buildings and finance teams, and they will probably continue as before. If there are still two congregations, once again those teams remain as before, but if there is now another congregation, there will need to be a third service-planning team. Similarly, there will probably be additional home groups, children's groups and so forth, so the adult nurture, children's nurture and pastoral teams will probably have grown too big and some kind of division into new teams will need to take place.

In total, the church may now have ten or twelve teams, but the overall leadership structure remains the same because the principle of CM is not size-dependent. As individual group leaders collaborate in the organization of ministry within agreed boundaries, each area of ministry collaborates with every other area of ministry across the church. Just as CM is suitable for both initially small and large churches, it can grow (or shrink) with any individual church while the various dynamics between the minister, leaders and members remain the same.

Secondly, how is a new area of ministry incorporated into a CM structure? Sometimes it is obvious where a new initiative fits. For example, perhaps the church decides to provide a lunch club for older residents. Depending on the aim of this ministry (is it to pastor, to teach, to meet need or what?), it could be added to either the pastoral or the adult nurture team. The lunch club leader (or another representative) would then join that team and the new ministry would trace its authority there. On other occasions, a new initiative doesn't seem to fit anywhere. Perhaps, for example, the church decides to open its doors between midnight and 2 o'clock at weekends as a safe haven for drunken youths. This is a new ministry, so it will probably need its own team—which is simply added to the existing structure, with a job description, a church council rep and a team leader who joins the team leaders' team. In this way, the new ministry would trace its authority to the team leaders' team, just like the existing teams.

CM is helpful in this process because, in order to establish where a new ministry fits into the overall ministry of the church, it asks 'What is the aim of this ministry?' In this latter case, the answer might be, 'Actually, we think that God might be asking us to form a youth congregation', in which case the weekend drop-in team would probably become a constituent group, with its leader or representative on a new youth nurture or youth congregation team (bridging the gap between the children's and adult nurture teams or adding to the service-planning teams).

THE PRACTICE OF CM

CM is an expression of the authority of Christ, the gifting of the Spirit and the parity of church membership. By organizing leadership into teams, four practical results are achieved:

- Each existing leader gathers with other leaders who are working in the same area of ministry, to pray, think and make decisions. Christians share ministry together under the authority of Christ.
- New leaders and potential leaders gather with existing leaders in order to listen to Christ and take responsibility for decisions made. Mentoring and the development of ministerial gifts given by the Spirit take place.
- For the ministry of the church to be shared in this way, faith is necessary.
- The church responds to the headship of Christ as some areas of ministry cease, others continue and others begin. This makes it possible (and probable) that, over a period of time, leaders will work hard in one area of ministry for a few years and then move into a different area. CM assists this personal development.

CM is not only concerned with leaders. Any structure of leadership is important because individual leaders usually mirror the leadership style of the whole organization. Therefore, when a church is pyramidal, even those at the lowest level of leadership tend to lead and minister in a pyramidal way. Experience shows that once leaders share ministry together in a CM structure, their style of leadership changes. They tend to lead and minister collaboratively (encouraging the activity of the Spirit that they see in others and encouraging ministry in those who receive it). In this way, leaders and members gather together around Christ in a non-hierarchical, new covenant way.

In the process of moving from pyramidal leadership to CM, setting up Collaborative Leadership is the first step. Once it is established, pyramidal leadership disappears from the structure altogether, because the theology of CM provides a different understanding of how leaders and members relate to one another, and the reality of this different approach is modelled by the behaviour and attitudes of the leaders. CM is not so much the practice of theory as the practice of theology.

Chapter 14

CHANGES FOR THE MINISTER

In terms of the CM timetable, the first few months are spent considering the theology and the historical structures, running the workshop and producing team job descriptions. Inevitably, this means extra work for the minister and for every leader involved in the process. By the end of the first year, however, teams are up and running, the minister and people are working together in ministry, and authority has been shared as many of the red and green lines that used to connect with the minister now connect to the teams. As the church begins to operate CM, the minister's role will change as he actively climbs down from the pinnacle of the pyramid. This will probably mean that he leaves a position which was comparatively isolated in order to be among (to collaborate with) not only leaders but also members. This change will most likely affect the following areas:

- Activity
- Knowledge
- Permission
- Authority
- Relationships

ACTIVITY

In the pyramidal structure, the minister delegates work and shoulders responsibility. In CM, both the work and the responsibility are shared across the church. Using our contemporary idea of family as an image, pyramidal leadership is like being the parent of small children: it fosters dependency. CM is like being the parent of children who have grown up, moved away and begun their own families: it promotes partnership. It's worth noting that moving from pyramidal leadership to CM can be emotionally difficult for both leaders and members because it is akin to adult children establishing their independence.

A great deal of the pyramidal minister's time is gobbled up in providing for the church. As the church grows in numbers, he will probably need assistance, so an administrator may be appointed. This will enable more to be done but will not remove the task of administration from the minister, because the work is delegated by him and he is responsible for it. The larger the church, the more time the minister will spend in meetings, because provision for the congregation, along with green and red lines of authority, comes from and to him.

Once a church moves into CM, much of this previously centralized administration will be shared out among the teams. This may mean that while the work done by the administrator does not necessarily change, the administrator now engages with a number of people instead of just one. This may take some careful initial management and possibly some reassessment of how the church uses its resources. In the same way, now that others are shouldering real responsibilities, significant decisions previously made only by the minister will be made in the teams. Also, tasks that were previously the minister's alone will probably be done by others, and this may also apply to pastoral contacts.

The minister will probably retain some aspects of administration, because he too will be active in a team (or two) and will take his proper share of the ongoing provision needed if the church is to both 'go out' and 'build up'. He will also, no doubt, have specific responsibilities commensurate with his task and will continue various personal contacts. The idea of CM is not that everyone in the church works hard except for the minister; the idea is that all collaborate according to their gifting, with a contribution appropriate to their circumstances. Having said all that, however, the first change that CM is likely to bring is to the minister's diary. He may find that whereas previously it was full, it is now comparatively empty. For years, he may have been complaining about being too busy and wishing he had more time to engage in aspects of ministry that he has long felt to be neglected. He may have taken on extra staff to help out, only to find that he is busier than ever (because this additional work has been delegated and the minister is therefore responsible for it). Now, as CM begins in the church, he finds that his diary has large chunks of space. Like a parent who watches the children leaving to make their own homes, he may feel very insecure and say, 'But what do I do now?' The answer, of course, is 'Whatever it was that God called you into ministry for in the first place!'

If the minister is a gifted evangelist, then he should engage in the 'going out' ministry of the church. If he is a gifted teacher, then he should teach. If he is a gifted pastor, then he should put his time and energy into this aspect of ministry (1 Peter 4:7–11). As soon as the church engages in CM, the minister becomes like everyone else. He continues his share of the administration, but this will be a fraction of what he did before. Now that the church is providing for itself, he can, together with everyone else, contribute to the work of God in the area. This may involve resurrecting a ministry killed off by busyness, developing a ministry that has been neglected, or beginning something new.

KNOWLEDGE

The pyramidal minister knows about everything that is going on in the church. This is a by-product of delegation. The CM minister, however, does not. He knows about what is going on in the teams to which he belongs, but he (like everyone else) knows only what he needs to know about what's going on in the other teams. He will need to develop an early strategy for dealing with requests for information. When someone asks, 'What time does the church picnic start?' it is not helpful for the minister to answer, 'Er… what picnic?' It's more helpful to reply, 'Can I just ask, do you know who's organizing it?' This question will probably be greeted with 'Oh, the toddler group' or such like, to which the minister can reply, 'Good. Look, give me your number and I'll get someone from toddlers to give you a ring with the details.' The CM minister soon learns to read the weekly news-sheet!

We may laugh at this change, but in reality it is significant and can cause friction. People expect the minister to know everything because he always has known everything. When he doesn't, it may cause irritation or even an angry outburst: 'Well, this is ridiculous! What sort of church is this when the minister hasn't got a clue what's going on?' What this reveals is simply the insecurity of change. It is also possible that the minister will struggle with this change. He may feel insecure about what's going on (that he doesn't know about), so, with empty spaces in his diary and the feeling that he is not in the thick of new initiatives, he may need a little tender loving care.

PERMISSION

Once the new teams begin to initiate ministry, CM really starts to have an impact on the minister. In the past, all initiatives and events were probably under his control, because that is what delegation and responsibility mean. Now, various teams will initiate events that the minister is dubious about. Some of them may sound to him like very bad ideas, and others (as he knows from experience) will seem doomed to failure. He cannot see how these initiatives can succeed and in the past he would have said 'No' to them. The events are the product of team decisions, however, and have been reached after prayer and discussion. For the minister to step in and stop them would be akin to a parent marching into their grown-up child's home, noisily demanding that the child redecorate their house so that it's like their parental home. The partnership of CM involves trust, so the planned initiatives and events must proceed.

Such new initiatives will have one of three outcomes:

- The event is a disaster. The minister was right—it was a bad idea.
- The event is wonderful. The team was right—it was a great idea.
- The event is mediocre. Everyone was wrong—it was neither bad nor good.

Whatever the outcome, there are lessons to be learned. The important difference in CM is that people learn these lessons together. Whereas, in the past, the opinion of the minister carried enormous weight, now his voice is one among many. He might be right or wrong, but his opinion is no more influential than any individual opinion because decisions are now corporate.

This change takes some getting used to. A CM minister may be tempted to exert his authority in order to influence decisions, and some people may willingly collude with him, reverting to pyramidal leadership and abrogating responsibility. In the early stages of CM, the minister will need to be proactive in his support of the decisions taken by teams, encouraging them when they both succeed and fail. The key to this is for everyone to understand that success reflects the leadership of Jesus Christ, not the minister or any individual leader—and failure is the spur to apology and perhaps repentance. If the minister shares the success, then he does so alongside every one else, because ultimately the whole congregation is seeking to follow Jesus Christ and listen to the voice of the Spirit. Getting an initiative wrong is only a problem if nothing is learned from the mistake; getting it right leads to praise and thanksgiving; either way, it leads to personal maturity.

AUTHORITY

It has already been noted that CM does not remove the need for a minister, and his ministry not only finds a focus in his personal gifting but is focused in his authority. This can be initially confusing because in pyramidal structures authority and responsibility tend to be regarded as the same thing. Because both are vested in the top man, they appear to describe slightly different facets of the same role. In fact, authority and responsibility are not the same and can be separated.

- Responsibility means accountability, liability, duty, and has overtones of blame and guilt.
- Authority means power, influence, right, and has overtones of ability and having the 'last word'.

The pyramidal minister has authority over the whole church and also responsibility for it. A CM minister also has authority over the church, even though much of it is shared, but responsibility rests with the church. This takes a good deal of getting used to because, at first glance, a CM church gives the impression the minister has given away his authority. In fact, he has not: he has shared his authority and given away responsibilities.

Let's envisage a CM church in which the minister is pastorally gifted: we will presume that he is a member of the pastoral team as well as being chair of the church council. When this minister chairs the church council, he exercises appropriate responsibility. In this area of the church's ministry, the buck stops with him because he is the chair. In the pastoral team, however, he shares responsibility with other team members: only if he is the team leader does the buck stop with him. He carries no responsibility at all in the youth team or the adult nurture team (and so forth) because he is not actively involved with those teams. This is not a delegated structure but a partnership under the authority of Christ, and demonstrates the heart of CM leadership: although responsibility is given away, authority is shared, and it is only shared in as much as the minister shares it. Ultimately, authority remains his. This can be most clearly seen in the arena of church discipline.

If a disciplinary matter cannot be resolved by an individual team or by team leaders, it is then referred to the minister. He does not take over the relevant ministry or make decisions that override the leaders involved, because they retain their responsibility. He works with them on the task, but on the issue of discipline the minister appropriately exercises authority. 'Discipline' can be thought of as a usually invisible team, which comes under the minister's remit. To put it another way, exercising this kind of authority is part of the minister's task.

In practice, this means that certain decisions can only be made by the minister—for example, how to handle situations when church leaders fall out. He can choose to deal with it alone or in collaboration with others. Just as the minister will probably be the chair of the church council, and possibly lead a ministry team, he is also leader of the 'discipline team' that tackles heresy and deals with bad behaviour. When called upon, this invisible team reveals itself as the minister deals with the situation either on a person-to-person level or by including others in the process. The minister retains this kind of authority under Christ, and the more he engages in CM, the more he will come to trust the insights and discernments that come from corporate decisions. After a few years of CM, the minister will often refrain from exercising his ministerial authority without first submitting his intentions to the discernment of others. A central theology of CM is that when two or three gather, the Lord Jesus Christ is present: therefore, in a corporate ministry the voice of the Spirit is listened to with others.

RELATIONSHIPS

Pyramidal ministers are often cautious about making personal friends within the church in case this is misinterpreted as favouritism on their part or as self-seeking flattery by members. In CM, everything changes because the minister is one clay jar among other clay jars (2 Corinthians 4:7). The treasure contained within the minister will encourage others and his gifts will be highly regarded, but he and his gifts will not be confused. He is free to admit to areas in which he struggles, and is able to show weakness (even personal disaster) because none of this detracts from the treasure or the gifting.

In addition, the minister is now working with others as colleagues. Friendship with the minister is no longer an escalator to influence: those who hunger for power might seek it by serving with a team (where they find that because every decision and much ministry is corporate, there is no personal power to be had and that it is God who gets the credit). Friendship with the minister or his family is therefore just like any other friendship in the church.

This, again, is a significant change that takes a bit of getting used to. The minister is no longer the role, but a person in his own right. Some people will like him and some won't, but this is irrelevant to the task. The task is to follow Christ, and the minister exercises his authority to encourage this following by helping the church to engage in CM. If a few people get to know and like the minister along the way, so much the better—after all, it is his church too.

For the CM minister, time spent in 'up front' ministry in the church and elsewhere remains much the same, and more time is spent in meetings than previously, but these are times when colleagues report, discuss, plan and pray. Preparation time is also much the same, but overall administration will have shrunk considerably, leaving time for his personal ministry of evangelism, teaching, pastoral care, youth work or whatever he is gifted for. In some denominations, part of this ministry comes to him (in the form of weddings, funerals, baptisms, personal disasters and so forth), but in any church, some of this ministry will be individual (for example, if the minister develops a counselling ministry) and some of it will be corporate (when he includes other church members in the ministry). In the process, he will probably make friends with a number of people because they are now colleagues together.

Each minister will develop a different personal ministry but the same overall division of 'diary time' will remain. For every minister, too, both meetings and personal ministry can be corporate activities in the New Testament sense, enabling him to make personal relationships with others.

HOME AND FAMILY

It is by no means uncommon for a minister to develop a 'double reputation'. He is highly thought of by the church and the neighbourhood because he always makes time for everyone. His family, however, are of a different opinion, because he never seems to be at home. In a pyramidal structure, losing personal space and family time is often one of the costs to the minister of church growth. The equation is simple: the bigger the church, the more is demanded of the pinnacle leader. Once CM is in place, the minister can use some of his newly available diary space to make his personal and spiritual life a higher priority, and more time may be allocated to prayer. Whether the minister is single or married, has children or a large extended family, then there will be more time to spend with friends, spouse and family. This is the last but by no means the least important change that CM can bring.

CM may also mean changes for the minister's spouse (if the minister is married). In a pyramidal structure, the spouse often assumes an automatic role in the life of the church, which some spouses relish and others hate. In CM, however, the minister's spouse (and children if he has them) become ordinary members of the congregation. Their leadership role (if they have one) will be dependent on their gifting, and they, like everyone else, can concentrate on whatever aspect of ministry they are called to. Role is not confused with task, friendship is understood and there is the freedom to explore new avenues of ministry.

To sum up, CM inaugurates significant changes in the life of any minister. What they do, what they know and their relationships with others will all change. Their social and family life will become more focused, and there will be increased space for personal development and spirituality. In short, in a CM church, the minister is neither isolated by his role nor alone in the task of ministry.

Chapter 15

CHANGES FOR THE CHURCH

In a CM church, everyone begins to take responsibility for both the 'building up' and the 'going out' functions. There is no longer an expectation that one person (the minister) will engage in every task; neither is there an expectation that a few people will do everything on behalf of everyone else. Instead, each person contributes to the overall task according to their gifting. In terms of ministry, whether this is expressed in word or action, every Christian stands with Christ in the gateway between the spiritual and the physical (as described in Chapter 6) and shares the task of mediation. When any Christian brings the needs of others to God (for example, through prayer), they are sharing in the priestly task. Similarly, when a Christian shares the concerns of God with other people (for example, through discussion), whether those people are fellow church members or strangers to the Christian faith, this too is priestly activity.

When a church changes its pattern of leadership, it is usually the leaders who are most profoundly affected. When a church engages with CM, however, every member of the church is affected, because CM describes the whole church, not just the leaders. The minister retains an authoritative role (under Christ) appropriate to his task as church leader, but the traditional multifaceted priestly task that was previously connected with that role is shared by the priesthood of all believers. Therefore, leaders do not collaborate with each other in order to minister to or on behalf of church members; they collaborate in leadership in order that the whole church might collaborate in ministry. This means that there are significant expectations of every member, and significant changes for them.

SHARING IN BUILDING UP

In a pyramidal structure, the task of building up the church and church members is the responsibility of the minister. When this task is shared, there will be changes to the understanding, tasks and workload of everyone.

In CM, each individual is trusted to exercise their gifts, but responsibility for how they are exercised is collaborative. Therefore, the offering of ministry is personal to the individual, but the discernment and management of it is corporate. This is a big change for any church, because traditional ministry is exercised on the basis of role. In pyramidal leadership, it's important to be a minister, a church officer, a group leader and so forth, because these roles provide the platform for ministry. In pyramidal structures, role and task are inseparable. In human terms, this can be positive because people tend to 'own' roles and work hard at any task that they regard as 'theirs'. The negative aspect is that when task and role are interdependent, it becomes difficult to criticize performance without criticizing role—in other words, hard to criticize the ministry without criticizing the minister. In CM, role and task are separated, ministry belongs to Christ and gifting may therefore be criticized in both the positive and negative senses (that is, discerned) without that criticism being perceived by default as a criticism of the individual. The community gathers around the task to discern the will of Christ and the whole process becomes objective.

It's useful to look at the gift of teaching as an example. Because it is linked with leadership (1 Timothy 3:2), teaching will offer many ministers an immediate opportunity to model CM in the way they exercise this gift. Also, if others in the church are gifted to teach, the dynamic of who exercises the gift (and on which occasions) can eloquently explain the separation between gifts and roles. In a traditional pyramidal structure, teaching tends to be valued highly and questioned rarely. In CM, there are two attitudes that apply to this gift (as to any other), which can be found in 1 Corinthians 12:7–11 and 14:26–33.

The teaching is not the teacher: The teacher is the same 'distance' from Christ as those who are taught, and everyone is equally under the authority of Jesus. The task of the teacher is therefore not to 'tell' others, but to 'share' a particular understanding. The teacher has a teaching gift and should use it, but he is not a ventriloquist's dummy; he collaborates with the Spirit when he shares his understanding. The teacher may have small or large spiritual fruit, but his gifting is another matter. Because God works incarnately, the teacher's words are a collaboration with the Holy Spirit and will probably contain something of God and something of the teacher. This is one practical outworking of the theology that the Holy Spirit speaks to the heart as the teacher speaks to the ear (see Chapter 5). Perhaps good teaching can be defined as 60 per cent collaboration between the teacher and the Spirit and 40 per cent of the teacher's own personal opinions. A bad sermon might then be explained as 2 per cent godly understanding and 98 per cent of the teacher's own agenda! Therefore, those who listen (the community) need to discern. Is what is being taught right? What is of God and what is of the teacher? This is a group activity to which all contribute. The whole congregation (including the teacher) gathers around the teaching and comes to a common mind about it. If something is not right, then everyone needs to know (especially the teacher). This is a big change for a CM church: members who previously accepted teaching without question are now expected to think for themselves; they carry equal responsibility with the teacher in the process of discerning the word of God.

Teaching is corporate: Because God gives gifts in order to work through them, reception is as important as transmission. If the teaching is godly, then the Christian community should put it into practice (James 1:22). If the church does not 'do' the word, good teaching can become spiritual entertainment. Over time, teachers will then tend to become discouraged, stop listening to God and teach just to fill a gap in the church's timetable.

Every spiritual gift can be approached with the same attitude. In CM, the ministry is not confused with the minister, because everyone is on level ground. Everyone has good days and bad days, and this is understood because everyone exercises gifts of ministry themselves and is used to the experience. All are used to working in partnership, collaborating together. No one is on a pedestal, no one is elevated above anyone else; all are together under one authority (Christ), sharing new life together by the one Spirit.

Leadership is approached in exactly the same way. It is a gift given so that God can work in and through the church. Leadership, however, is not the leader; it's just another gift. It may be exercised well or badly, but it is a corporate activity and open to scrutiny and discernment.

In a traditional pyramidal church, differences of opinion tend to take the form of negative criticism, and when the motive is mischievous the criticism is done from a safe distance. In CM, criticism is replaced by discernment—which is close up and personal, because it involves declaring opinions openly. Thus, each member's insights are taken seriously and either agreed with or disagreed with, which can take some getting used to.

Concentrating ministry

Once a CM structure is established, another issue will surface. It will be impossible for any individual to be involved everywhere. In fact, for any church member who has a life (a job, family, friends and interests), it is unlikely that they will have the time to engage with more than one team, or possibly two. This may provoke a whole shift in church culture, if the ten people who previously did everything concentrate on areas that they are gifted for and the remaining church members begin to do more than they ever imagined. For some people, the shift may prove unwelcome. Some of the original ten important people may resent others doing their jobs and feel a consequential loss of status. This is an inevitable effect of separating task from role. Also, some members of whom much is now expected may resent having to do anything at all. Whether the shift is welcomed or not, however, a basic premise of CM is that everyone is involved in ministry, and the success or failure of CM will ultimately depend on the church's willingness to be under the authority of Christ.

As a by-product of separating role and task, any church that implements CM will probably face the loss of the 'superstar'. CM works with jars of clay, not golden pots, and while some golden pots may be relieved to lose their shine (revealing the clay beneath), others may wish to retain it. These people tend to leave and join another church where they feel that they can 'shine' appropriately. Although the process of losing certain existing leaders may be draining, the discovery of treasure in every clay jar more than makes up for it.

Relocating power

A significant change for a CM church will be to the role of the church council (or church elders, or whatever the relevant decision-making body is called). In a pyramidal structure, its members often hold substantial power, because it is the one arena in which the people can challenge the minister. Once a church embarks on CM, this body will change, because much of the business that was previously done by the council is now done elsewhere. Never again will the central decision-making body spend an hour discussing the colour of the service sheets, the behaviour of the Sunday school children or the recent home group course. All of these issues (along with a hundred others) are now dealt with in the teams. In a similar fashion to the minister, the church council may look at its seemingly empty agenda and say, 'But what do we do now?'

It may be tempting to dissolve the church council (or equivalent body) quietly, but this would be a mistake. In the Church of England, for example, the council is a legal requirement, and experience shows that its existence can be turned to advantage. Each of the new teams focuses specifically on an area of ministry, and the team leaders' team enables whole-church communication and planning. The council can become the one body in the church that:

- Makes final decisions corporately.
- Makes final decisions regarding the brief and scope of each team.
- Engages with whole-church vision.
- Balances 'going out' with 'building up'.

In other words, the council is the place where vision crystallises. This is very important, because in a CM church it is not the minister alone who receives and disseminates vision. Vision, like every other aspect of ministry, is corporate. Each council member belongs to a team and they are aware of what God is doing in that area of ministry, so this gathering has the opportunity to gather around the risen Christ and get some sense of the complete ministry (wonders, gaps, warts and all). Without a church council of some sort, a CM church may attend to the parts and forget the whole.

The answer to the question 'What do we do now?' is this: 'Listen to the Spirit and share with the church what you hear.' In this change of role, some people will decide that the council is no longer the place for them, and they will contribute to a team. Other people will sigh with relief and relish the new task. Yet others will serve for the first time on the council, probably to their surprise, and (as always) a few people will yearn for the past.

An increase of accredited ministry

Because ministry is shared in a CM church, much of it becomes 'bite-sized'. Previously, a few multitalented people displayed breathtaking gifts; now, lots of ordinary people add their personal puff to the wind of the Spirit. In pyramidal structures, church members tend to look at their leaders and say, 'I could never do that!' In CM, the people tend to think, 'Look at what so-and-so is doing… I wonder if I could do that too.' For them it's then a short step to thinking, 'I wonder if God is asking me to do that.' At the same time, their gifting is often recognized by others working alongside them and, with encouragement, training begins—within the church, with a nationally accredited body, through a denominational scheme or through a Christian training course. Thus, accredited ministry (which some churches refer to as vocations) in CM is incremental; the leap of faith is the same, but the task is manageable. The gap between the talented and the ordinary has narrowed because there are no golden pots, only clay jars. In the CM environment, it isn't long before accredited ministry begins to emerge across the church, and the journey from finding faith to exercising leadership may be comparatively short. This is one practical outworking of the point made in Chapter 10: if the CM soil is healthy, the leadership crop will grow.

As these ministries come to light, the corporate nature of CM allows them to be tested, because even the smallest gift can be exercised somewhere. In a pyramidal structure, engaging in ministry often involves a large step up towards the top, fulfilling delegated responsibilities. In CM, ministry involves working with others and blending gifts into the mix. It also means that individuals learn to exercise their gifts interdependently with others, which tends to keep the focus on the task, on Christ, and off self.

This rise in accredited ministry brings an important change to the church. In a pyramid, the availability of leadership posts is commensurate with the shape of the whole. In other words, there is only one top spot, a few deputy posts, a few more head-of-department posts, many more leader posts, and so on. The further down the pyramid one goes, the more leadership posts there are. This means that a pyramid is always looking for 'lower rank' leaders, while the 'higher rank' posts rarely become vacant. If someone in the church is gifted for higher rank, then they will probably need to leave and find another church with a vacancy. In CM, however, the focus is on gifting. If there are 20 gifted leaders in one area of ministry and only two people gifted in another, then the shape of the church develops according to the leaders. The attitude is, 'Now, how and where can we use your ministry?' rather than 'Ah, sorry, other people are doing that already, so why not do this instead?' This is the theology of Christ's authority in practice. If he is the head of the body, and if he gives ministerial gifts, then the ultimate shape of the church is up to him.

This model of leadership and ministry then feeds back into the body of the church. When gifts are exercised, CM provides a secure environment to determine whether they should be encouraged or reined in—because all ministries are open to scrutiny. Over a period of time, gifting may emerge in a previously ignored area of ministry, but even when this does not happen CM prevents individuals from getting stuck in the same rut for decades and confirms all activity as vocational.

SHARING IN GOING OUT

Although 'going out' ministry is not strictly the subject of this book, it must at least be mentioned. Sharing the good news about Christ in both word and deed is central to a CM church if it is to be outward-looking. The changes and principles already noted apply not only to 'building up' ministries, but also to evangelism, mission, care for the needy and every other facet of ministry that we recognize as 'going out'. There is one beneficial difference in a CM church, however.

In a pyramidal structure, the style of ministry tends to echo the style of leadership. Therefore, when the church builds up, it tends to present the gospel in a delegated fashion ('this was given to me, and now I give it to you'). In a CM structure, Christians get used to sharing the gospel together, and are used to having it discerned (that is, questioned). This means that when CM church members go out, they tend not to 'deliver truth' but to share insight, experience and belief. There is also the recognition that in both personal meetings and large events, the dynamic or shape of the encounter is identical to the leadership structure—individuals gathered together around Christ. This means that a CM church tends to think of 'going out' ministry in terms of introduction—not to the church, but to Jesus Christ—and expects to collaborate with the Holy Spirit in the process. Thus, ministry echoes leadership, and lessons learnt in one arena tend to be applied in the other.

RIGHT HERE, RIGHT NOW

CM is appropriate to any culture, whether it is community-based or, like ours, individualistic. In our society, CM offers four values that are immediately understood:

- These days, people approach politics through single issues (the environment, health care, education and so forth). In a CM church, a variety of individuals minister in different areas, so people find a way into church by aligning themselves with the aspect of ministry closest to their hearts.
- Because the leadership structure is flat, many people warm to a minister who is 'one of us'.
- Because there is trust and responsibility, many people relish the entrepreneurial aspect to team leadership and ministry. Even newcomers can be encouraged to 'have a go'.
- Because the pinnacle person in each area of ministry is Christ, the church offers a gateway to the divine without presenting a 'hotline'

person in between. A spiritual experience is therefore offered through the body of Christ (in relationships) rather than through the ministry of a special individual.

In other words, whereas a pyramidal structure has, by default, a single point, the CM church is multifaceted, which enables a wide variety of people to identify with one body. This is clearly beneficial but it can also be a big change for the church. Previously, emphasis was probably placed on all pulling together on the same corporate rope—perhaps the next big project. Now, the expectation is that everyone will be shoulder to shoulder, getting on with the task in front of them. Thus, while the pyramidal church is epitomized by single, large projects, the CM church is epitomized by a multiplicity of small, often personal, ventures. A CM church is quite capable of initiating projects of every size, including large ones, and several or all teams join forces to do this, working on various aspects of the project as a joint venture. The tendency, however, is for the CM church to proliferate small projects, which can challenge traditional interpretations of the meaning of 'success', especially for those who relish the monumental and find it difficult to rejoice in the 'day of small things' (Zechariah 4:10).

In our culture, the multifaceted nature of CM is readily understood because it is perceived as individualism. In truth, it is not, but the community nature of it comes as a revelation, as does the immediacy of the Spirit. This means that in our society, where so many people are spiritual but without direction, CM casts a wide net.

GROWING LEADERS

For the church to function effectively, there must be leaders. In a pyramidal structure, the approach to finding leaders tends to be:

- Identify the task.
- Find a leader for it.
- Train and appoint them.
- Support them.

As the task begins, the new leader works within the level of responsibility delegated to them. In a CM structure, there are two different approaches to leadership:

1. Identify the task.
   - Gather a team of people to share the task.
   - The team appoints its own leader.
   - The church (perhaps the church council or team leaders) confirms the leader, and the leader is trained.
   - The team and the leader support each other.

2. Identify a number of people with similar gifting.
   - Gather them together to begin the task for which they are gifted.
   - The team appoints its own leader.
   - The church confirms the leader, and the leader is trained.
   - The team and the leader support each other.

Therefore, while the pyramidal minister approaches leadership by choosing individuals, the CM minister approaches leadership primarily through task. This is why, in Chapter 10, the CM minister was likened to a farmer who attends to the soil of the church in which the crop of ministry and leadership grows—as opposed to the pyramidal approach, in which individual attention is given to each plant (or leader). This difference in approach will probably impact on the CM church in two ways.

First of all, unlikely people may become leaders. Because their leadership is identified by the team, they may be people who have very different views from the minister's, and some may be people whom other churches would regard as uneducated, of poor social standing, the wrong age, and maybe even with a questionable personal history. In a pyramidal structure, for the minister to delegate responsibility to such people would be to take an enormous risk, because task equals role and these people would be given a perilously high platform in the church. In a CM church, however, these people are not given individual authority, responsibility or role. They simply lead the team for a time, or exercise their gifting within it, and they always share the ministerial task with others. In this way, people who elsewhere might be considered unsuitable for leadership are able to grow, develop and mature in faith and ministry. Similarly, other people who, from lack of personal confidence, would never previously have accepted a leadership role, do so. Sometimes, as in any church, this kind of leadership goes wrong, but because role and task are shared, so is risk, so any potential damage to either the ministry of the church or to the individual concerned is limited.

Secondly, because CM leadership is a bottom-up process, the church may be challenged about fundamental issues. For example, the focus of this challenge could be the attitude towards men and women in ministry. If the church has strong views about male leadership, what does it do if it embraces a CM theology and approach and then finds that the Holy Spirit gifts women for ministries that have previously been a male preserve? CM will not only change the leadership pattern; it will also confront the church with a range of issues that need to be addressed.

FOCUS ON FAITH

Everyone engaged in ministry in a CM church is entrusted with real responsibility but is expected to collaborate with God and with their fellow Christians to fulfil that responsibility. In other words, CM is a way of enabling every believer to become part of the new covenant priesthood. Having said that, does the personal holiness (or lack of it) of each 'priest' matter? When the church operates pyramidal leadership, priests (or whatever they are called in different churches) occupy the pinnacle and, because role and task are combined, spiritual gifts are expected to mirror spiritual fruit. The leaders are expected to be both gifted and fruity (or 'holy'). In a CM church, where role and task are separated, what happens when someone exhibits big gifts and small fruit?

In the New Testament, there are four hallmarks that identify Christian men and women. They can be found in Acts 2:

- Repent—which is commonly noted as 'believe' (v. 38a)
- Baptism (v. 38b)
- Gift of the Holy Spirit (v. 38c)
- Belong (vv. 41–47)

It doesn't seem to matter in which order these four hallmarks appear. For example, when Peter visits Cornelius in Acts 10 (see Chapter 5), the order seems to be: belong, believe, Holy Spirit, baptism. Similarly, for the Christians in Samaria (Acts 8:14–17) the order seems to be: believe, belong, baptism—gap—Holy Spirit, and for the Ephesian Christians (Acts 19:1–7): believe, belong—gap—baptism, Holy Spirit. The apostles do not judge this varying order in the sense of saying 'This is the right (or wrong) way to do things.' Instead, their concern is to ensure that all four hallmarks are present.

In a CM church, this approach will probably be applied to both 'going out' and 'building up' ministries. The attitude of church members to non-members, for example, is less likely to be of the black and white 'I believe; you don't' variety and more likely to be of the shades of grey sort—looking for hallmarks of faith already present and encouraging a completion of the process. This is, as it were, a collaborative approach to evangelism, in which the evangelist expects to co-operate with both the Spirit and the listener. But it is not a vague approach, because it expects growth and further experience and commitment.

The attitude to potential leaders will probably take the same principle and apply it to the presence of spiritual fruit, looking for a spiritual work in progress rather than present attainment. To put this bluntly, pyramidal churches tend to appoint to leadership only those who are regarded as already suitable (all fruit present and correct), whereas CM churches tend to appoint also those whose hearts are in the right direction (small fruit, but growing), even if they have a very long way to go. When believers stand in the gateway of priesthood, seeking to collaborate with one another and with Christ, the Spirit tends to shine a spotlight on personal shortcomings, so anyone who shares in ministry will experience significant personal growth as they learn to face problems by exercising their faith, dealing with failure as well as success. Ultimately, CM sharpens the focus on personal faith because the shared responsibility tests the reality of Christian belief.

In a CM church, what is true for CM leaders is equally true for church members. At its most fundamental level, because CM depends on the reality of Christianity, it reveals any gaps in faith, understanding or experience, and drives everyone to seek the face of Christ.

Chapter 16

CHALLENGES SPECIFIC TO COLLABORATIVE MINISTRY

As we have now made clear, CM seeks, at the most fundamental level, to collaborate with the Holy Spirit under the authority of Jesus Christ. As a structure, it includes everyone in the church, not just the leaders. It is very flexible because ministry is not dependent on the number of available leaders; instead, the membership of the church determines ministry. CM fosters maturity, releases gifts, shares ministry and encourages Christian fellowship. The disadvantage is that changing from pyramidal leadership to CM is very hard work, requiring changes in attitude, understanding and thinking. CM is not a management technique that can be implemented over the top of an existing pyramidal structure. To adopt it, a church must think collaboratively, and changing minds is a lot harder than giving people new leadership titles.

It would be dishonest to ignore the fact that there are some challenges specific to CM. It has already been noted that it does not accommodate 'superstar ministries', and some people find this impossibly difficult. Some love to bask in the reflected glory of their minister, like passengers who are particularly proud of their driver. Similarly, there are others who wish to be superstars themselves and cannot work with others in partnership. The change from pyramidal leadership to CM is so fundamental that some, like the Hebrews who crossed the Red Sea with Moses, will look back with longing to Egypt. Thus, when a church begins CM, it may be that some existing members, and leaders, decide to worship elsewhere. This can be a painful experience for all concerned and, behaving according to tradition, anger will probably be directed towards the perceived top man—the minister. For those who commit to CM, there are a number of challenges such as this to be aware of.

Many challenges can be regarded as either problems or opportunities. CM raises issues that different churches may regard as positive, negative or even neutral, but they will need attention.

BECOMING LIKE THE MINISTER

In CM, each area of ministry has a leader, assistant leaders, people and so forth—so it can be all too easy for team leaders to emulate the role of a pyramidal minister. At the apex of each team, though, is Jesus, not the team leader. Therefore, each team should follow the pattern of New Testament leadership. The leader's task is to co-ordinate and facilitate, not to rule or direct. When the focus is on God, the teams tend to mimic family relationships or friendships rather than secular work departments.

It should never be forgotten, however, that human nature is fallen. Therefore, the church must beware of leaders who 'lord it over' others. Dealing with this is easier if we remember that when leaders behave in this way it is usually because they are reverting to the past, when pinnacle leadership was the only model available.

DO AS I DO

This issue attaches firmly to the minister and will probably manifest itself in three different ways. First of all, in the early days of CM (when the minister is still deciding on the right ministry to fill the spaces in his diary), it may emerge in the guise of criticism: 'Don't get me wrong, this Collaborative Ministry is really good, but the minister gets paid for this and we don't, so shouldn't he be doing... the pastoral visiting, or heading up the building project—or whatever this person's main concern is?' This criticism is actually another way of saying, 'I don't want to do this!' The truth is that because of CM, the critic will grow—perhaps with a new vocation—as he engages with 'going out' ministry as well as with building up the church. Therefore, CM demands more of the critic, and if this encourages him to mature in Christ, then the minister is earning his keep.

Secondly, it is important for the minister to model CM. He does this in the early days by deliberately choosing a ministry or two in which he can either function as an assistant leader or as another pair of willing hands. For example, if the church is running a children's club, the minister could sign up as a group leader or assistant leader. Other leaders organize and run the day, and the minister does as he is told. Or perhaps the minister has musical gifts? Then he could join the church band or choir (if there is one), and once again be seen under the authority of others. Another example would be if the church were doing some chores—gardening or decorating—then maybe the minister could clear out the drains (or some equally glamorous job), which provides another opportunity to submit to the leadership of others. Or perhaps the minister can just sit in the congregation on Sunday, if he's not involved in leading worship. The opportunities will differ from church to church, but this kind of practical parable reinforces the meaning of CM and will be helpful when the minister is present at team meetings, but is not the team leader. The principle in CM is 'Do as I do', not just 'Do as I say', and, in the transition between the pyramid and CM, the actions of the minister will speak volumes.

Thirdly, this issue will probably manifest itself through authority. Sooner or later, an individual or group will confuse responsibility with authority, and start behaving as a pinnacle person, declaring that they have a hotline to God. Because the minister is occupying the level ground of collaboration, this person or group will think that he has no authority. At this point, the invisible 'discipline team' (mentioned in Chapter 14) is revealed, and the person or group will discover the difference between authority and responsibility as the whole church stands calmly with the minister. The point is that the New Testament does not differentiate the tasks of 'bishop, priest and deacon' for fun, and the attitude that if CM operates in every church, then there won't be the need for so many ministers, is frankly mistaken. Even though CM may deceive the uneducated eye into thinking that the minister is redundant, he needs to be there. His task is to ensure that disciples follow their master, and he has the authority to do this.

GETTING MOANED AT

Every minister knows what it's like to get moaned at. In a pyramidal structure, the minister will receive most of the serious moaning, while ordinary church members experience only grumbles. Once a church engages in CM, the moaning is redirected towards a large number of people (team leaders in particular). This can come as a shock to those who are on the receiving end of moaning for the first time, and it can lead to serious doubt, along the lines of 'So-and-so has just moaned at me; my efforts must be poor quality; this never used to happen when talented people were in charge; I'm useless and CM doesn't work!'

In actual fact, two different things are happening at the same time. First, in the past, when the 'talented people' were in charge, so-and-so used to moan at them, but they probably kept those negative conversations confidential. The team leader doesn't know that the moan has just been redirected. Second, the team leader thinks that the 'talented people' were never moaned at because the team leader never saw any reason to moan at them. No ministry is judged by the yardstick of moaning, except perhaps by an inverse ratio (consider, for example, the ministry of Jesus, Paul, Peter or anyone else in the Bible), and moaning most certainly is not a reason to throw in the CM towel.

To manage moaning is not difficult: it just takes love, courage and a bit of back-up. The beauty of CM is that it is corporate, so the back-up is built in. Whereas in pyramidal leadership moaning is a person-to-person pastime, in CM no individual should be on the receiving end. Therefore, others should be included (ideally, other team members). With two or three people as back-up, it is possible to be very loving and, by concentrating on the moan rather than on the moaner, one can, as it were, love the moaner while hating the moan. In God's economy, this is more straightforward when it is done corporately. Finally, it may be necessary to take the moans seriously, and make a decision: they may be unpleasant to listen to, but is the moaner right? If so, then change is in order; and if the moaner is wrong, it helps if they understand why that is the case. Once again, this seems easier to accomplish with several people, and if Jesus is in charge of this ad-hoc meeting, the outcome will very probably be positive for all concerned.

However moaning is dealt with, it will continue. In fact, when team leaders get moaned at, this affirms the CM structure, because the person complained to them rather than to the minister—so the red and green lines of authority and responsibility have been successfully shared. When this is pointed out, the team leader concerned can end up actually encouraged!

MAINTENANCE IS FUN

The early years of CM can feel like playing with a corporate train set: now everyone gets to change the points, not just the minister. Engaging with ministry is such a journey of discovery that if care is not exercised, a church can have so much fun building up that it neglects to go out. Even worse, it may be tempted to set up an outreach team to focus on this aspect of ministry. Experience shows that this can be a mistake. Once a CM church has such a team, the tendency is for the rest of the membership to leave evangelistic mission to the team. It is far better to seed 'going out' activities through the whole structure so that every aspect of ministry carries the same expectation.

Maintenance is fun. It is helpful to remember, though, that while it's important to build up disciples, it's not necessary to get every detail of church life right. For as long as groups, activities and so forth fulfil their remit, the church runs them; when they cease to do so, they are pruned. In a nutshell, a CM church should try to maintain only what needs maintaining, and avoid getting so focused on reorganizing current activities that going out and new work is ignored.

CHANGE FEELS LIKE GROWTH

This point follows on from maintenance being fun. The change from pyramidal leadership to CM involves so many people that it can feel like growth. In one sense, it is, because individuals mature and grow and vocations develop. In a CM church, however, enlargement can be mistaken for expansion. To use the image of a contemporary family, the children may have got bigger, but there are still the same number of them.

Whether the church grows numerically has little to do with the style of ministry. Some pyramidal churches grow healthily and others don't. The same is true for CM, which frankly gives the lie to assumptions that CM leads to numerical growth. CM certainly promotes numerical growth and provides a splendid structure within which growth can take place, but whether any individual church adds to its numbers is down to the attitude of individual members, not to the leadership structure.

To put this as bluntly as possible, if the church goes out, it will grow; if it doesn't, it won't. The word 'church' in this context means the minister, church leaders, church members, you, me, all of us. In CM it's wise to acknowledge that change can be deceptive, because it can feel like growth when it isn't.

CHANGING SHAPE

Because CM is a bottom-up system that looks for gifting, it is not possible to predict which ministries will arise, and it is therefore impossible to predict the future shape of the church. Most Christians tend to approach church with a traditional view, expecting standard provision for both adults and children with a mixture of social and worship settings. Thus, in pyramidal structures, there is always an awareness of areas of church life that are perceived as gaps or potential failings. In CM, the shape of the church is dependent on the membership, which means, for example, that if there are no children's leaders, then there will be no children's work. The church might want it and pray for it, but unless the Spirit gifts people for the ministry, the church won't have it. This aspect of CM can come as something of a shock, but the theology of CM expects that the Spirit will provide gifts for the task. Therefore, if a neighbouring church has gifted children's leaders, maybe they should be ministering with children, not us? Perhaps we should develop ministry with the elderly instead? CM churches tend to view neighbouring churches as colleagues rather than rivals. Also, because CM churches engage in ministry corporately, they tend not to import professionals with the expectation that these leaders will minister in the members' stead; rather, members expect to work with them in a way that identifies and empowers their own gifting.

Once an individual church recognizes that it can't do everything, it's a short step to asking the pinnacle leader (Christ) exactly what it should be doing. This may reveal that some of the existing work should be pruned and energy directed elsewhere. Another facet of the same issue is having too many leaders. If a church embarks on CM with the idea that CM will prop up traditional church activities, a church may end up with too many leaders (and, as noted in the section concerning accredited ministry in the previous chapter, probably in all of the wrong departments). For example, what happens if a church commits to CM because it thinks that this style of leadership will provide more people to share in the task of pastoral visiting, and the Spirit gifts ten preachers instead? Does the church try to retain its original shape by using preachers for a pastoral task or bite the bullet, admit that the pastoral task isn't going to get done and establish some extra teaching arenas instead? It helps to remember that many of the tasks the church engages in are not specifically mentioned in the New Testament at all: we are just told to go out and build up. In CM, the focus is on the activities for which we have leaders, even if (to our eyes) the church looks unbalanced. Fundamentally, the shape of our church is none of our concern; if Jesus is in charge, then we trust him to know what he is doing.

The final facet of this issue is particular to larger churches because it involves the demise of the traditional weekly staff meeting. The word 'staff' is usually used to mean those in full-time (probably paid) ministry and also specific high-ranking leaders. Even when there are a number of paid staff, once CM begins, the staff meeting will no longer be appropriate in its traditional form. Firstly, much of what this meeting used to achieve will now be done elsewhere in the teams. Secondly, the 'staff' will have increased in size (because it now includes every leader in the church), and many of these people probably work for a living and cannot attend such a meeting. Thirdly, the 'top people gathering around the top man' nature of the staff meeting is redundant because all of the staff now occupy the same level ground as everyone else.

Losing the staff meeting can be an emotional event for the former members. It can also flummox denominational overseers or outside parties who cannot understand how the 'staff' (meaning a few accredited leaders) can continue to function without this traditional meeting. Perhaps it is best just to recognize that the staff continue to gather around the top man, Jesus; it's just that they now do so with others, not only with each other.

LINE MANAGEMENT

This is another issue that is particularly sharp for larger churches in which the focus has traditionally been on the staff. In the Church of England, for example, the minister (vicar) line-manages the assistant minister (curate), and many churches employ an administrator. Thinking about the administrator first, one of the changes engendered by CM is the expansion of leadership. Is it possible for one person to have, say, twelve bosses? The answer is, of course, 'No', so it's important that team leaders and others understand who line-manages the administrator. It doesn't matter if this is the minister or someone else, as long as the administrator knows who is in charge of their task. Whether their work comes from one person or twelve will make little difference; what is needed is for someone to manage the flow.

There will probably be big changes to the administrator's role, however, if they have also been acting as personal assistant to the minister. A large percentage of this aspect of the administrator's task will now have been shared across the teams, and this means that a rewrite of their job description may be necessary. Whether the administrator will wish to 'change jobs' to this extent will determine whether he or she continues in post or leaves. If it all works out fine, and it is decided that the minister will line-manage the administrator, they must both be aware of the change. From the minister's point of view, this will become one of the areas of ministry in which he behaves as a team leader, by connecting with all those who pass work to the administrator and by making sure that suitable systems of communication are in place and working.

The assistant minister (the curate, or equivalent trainee post in another denomination) will also need to be considered. The minister will probably have no choice but to line-manage this person but, once again, CM will change the relationship. Often, the aim is for the assistant to be trained so that they can leave and become a minister in another church. In CM, training will involve mentoring rather than apprenticing, which means that the assistant won't shadow the minister all the time but the minister will make sure that the assistant's training is thorough by linking him or her with all of the leadership teams at one time or another. Instead of a staff meeting, a progress meeting may be more appropriate. CM doesn't mean that all one-to-one meetings cease; it just means that no task (or decision about any task) is undertaken entirely by any individual. Personal and private conversations remain confidential and, here again, the minister can think of this mentoring as an area of ministry in which he exercises both authority and responsibility. Thus, the minister can mentor the assistant minister even though they usually do not work together in the traditional sense. Both work together with the church and with Christ instead. Once again, this is a concept so far removed from pyramidal thinking that those who are not used to CM struggle with it.

Another aspect of management is communication. Experience shows that both verbal reports and written records are needed. Some meetings will need minutes (for example, the church council) but most will not. Because of the spread-out nature of the leadership, it is, however, very useful to keep a record of team decisions made (especially when they affect other teams). Experience also shows that paper records are in themselves insufficient, because the church is not a business and people tend not to read memos or plough through piles of paperwork. Keeping a note of decisions made enables team leaders, and others, to take some kind of reminder to meetings where verbal reporting is vital.

Surprisingly, the person for whom this practice may be most difficult is the minister. In the pyramid, other people always took the minutes when required, and in other meetings no record of decisions was needed. In CM, every meeting needs to be noted or decisions will be forgotten, inadvertently overruled or duplicated. For the minister in particular, this can be a big change. If he consistently forgets to do this, then some kind of system for managing the minister's memory will need to be established!

PREPARING THE SOIL

To get CM started, the minister will need to engage in hard labour, analogous to ploughing. Preparing the ground combines biblical teaching with practical action. Once this is done, however, and the seeds are planted, the minister scares off the crows, keeps the weeds down and waits while the crop begins to grow underground. Whereas pyramid leadership is hands on and directive, CM is hands off and trusting. The pyramidal minister keeps a close eye on the important individual plants—the leaders in whom he is investing particular care. The CM minister keeps a close eye on the ground instead, because if the soil is healthy the crop will be fine, and the church will flourish as gifting becomes plain, leaders arise and events and ministry take place.

Another way to express this order of priorities is to echo the intentions of the apostles who told the church that they would give their time to prayer and preaching. The minister can spend some of his time checking the soil and give the rest to the ministry for which he is gifted.

PATIENCE AND ORGANIZATION

In pyramidal leadership, decision-making is delegated to individuals; therefore, getting a decision is simply a matter of contacting the person concerned. In a CM church, because decision-making is shared, getting a decision might take longer. For example, in a pyramidal church, a home group member might have a bright idea for a teaching series, so they phone up the minister and get an answer straight away. In a CM structure, they explain their idea to their home group and the rep takes it to the adult nurture team for a decision—but maybe the team met last week and isn't scheduled to meet for another six weeks. This change can be a real challenge to some, and particularly to those who have previously enjoyed what they perceived to be a direct line to the very top.

Once a church moves into CM, everyone has to take responsibility for organizing themselves. This means that church members have to get used to thinking ahead so that they don't miss deadlines. Part of collaboration is keeping in step with others. On the other hand, situations and opportunities inevitably arise that need to be dealt with quickly, so what used to apply to the central church council or to the minister now applies to the teams. In other words, an exceptional, single-issue meeting might be needed, or a decision that is taken 'on the fly' by a leader will need ratifying by the team at a later date, through some form of 'confirmation of actions taken' procedure. For CM to be effective, however, both patience and organization will be needed.

USING CM FOR PERSONAL GAIN

If the minister or any other leader has a hidden agenda for the church, they may try to promote CM for personal gain. To focus on the minister as an example, in a pyramidal structure the success of the church is attributed to the minister because he delegates and manages ministry. From the minister's point of view, a 'success' looks good on his CV and anything else does not. So some ministers may see CM as a way of improving their personal CV, especially in a church environment where the word 'collaborative' has become widespread. Experience indicates, however, that this kind of personal agenda will tend to backfire. The only way to undertake CM is by submitting to the Lordship of Christ.

CM brings a cost for the minister and it may as well be acknowledged. Because ministry is shared, success is distributed and does not accrue to the minister's account. If any minister wants to build a career out of ministry, then CM will probably not accomplish this for him. The reward of CM will not be seen in the minister's CV but in the daily lives of the church members and the community they serve together.

WEIGHING IT UP

Overall, the biggest challenge of CM is that it requires a Jesus-centred approach to every task, and demands corporate discernment and action. To engage with God and with others requires everyone to swim out of their depth, and this stimulates prayer, even if it is choked out in its most rudimentary form: 'Help me—I'm drowning!'

Overall, the second biggest challenge of CM is that the church is constantly evolving. There is a certain irony to this challenge, given that most Christians wish to see the church continually changing for the better. A CM church, however, can never heave a sigh of relief and say, 'Well, that's our church sorted out then!' because the Spirit blows where he wills and brings change.

The Holy Spirit seems to ask every Christian generation the same two questions. The first is, 'Whose church is this?' For some, ownership of the church will be identified with a building, and the focus of this question will challenge its use and ordering. For others, ownership of the church will be identified with particular powerful organizations or individuals, and the focus of the question will challenge issues of personal power and influence. Those churches able to answer, 'It's your church, Lord Jesus!' experience a new freedom as buildings, organizations and individuals take their proper place under the authority of Christ. CM seeks to structure the church in this way.

The Spirit then asks a second question: 'If it's my church, may I have it back?' Essentially, CM is a way of saying, 'Yes'.

CONCLUSION

If God does not exist, or if God does not choose to be known, or if Jesus did not rise from the dead, or if he never sent his Spirit to enliven human beings—then CM will not work. If God does exist, wants to be known, raised Jesus from the dead and breathed his Spirit upon the church—it will. It is impossible to exercise CM without faith, because if Jesus is not in the centre, there is no leader, and if the Spirit does not gift for ministry, the church has nothing to offer.

This model of church keeps every Christian where they should be—under the authority of the living God, nose down in the dirt before the throne of grace; but, astonishingly, raised up by that grace and, incredibly, entrusted with the gifts of ministry. These gifts are then exercised on level ground alongside every other church member.

As we have seen in this book, CM is quintessentially different from pyramidal leadership. It has a different theology, holds different attitudes and treasures different values. People in a CM church relate to one another in a different way, and CM leaders operate only in community. CM is neither a management technique nor a facet of delegation: it is the organic, incarnational living out of New Testament promise, given life by the presence of the Holy Spirit. The expression of CM in each church will be individual and different from every other church. CM, therefore, cannot be bolted on to existing pyramidal leadership structures, and it will not directly solve two contemporary problems—fewer ministers and smaller congregations.

In this book, we have considered present, traditional and historical leadership structures in Part One. We have attended to the theology of leadership and defined CM in Part Two, and in Part Three we have looked at the practicalities and challenges of ministering collaboratively. CM offers a structure and an opportunity from which to address the problems of fewer ministers and smaller congregations, but it will solve them only if we rise to the primary challenge of being human, and give back to God that which belongs to him: Lordship.

At the most fundamental level, we should never in engage in CM because we think it will solve contemporary problems. We should only engage in CM if we believe it is the right way to be church.

BIBLE STUDY NOTES

The following pages are copyright free and may be reproduced in any format, provided that the source is acknowledged (David Robertson, *Collaborative Ministry*, BRF, 2007). These Bible study notes are designed to be used by small groups, but they do not stand alone and will need to be used in conjunction with Part Two of this book (Chapters 5–11). It is anticipated that the group leader will consider these chapters, and then use the following notes when leading group discussion.

The first chapter in Part Two (Chapter 5: Some lessons from Acts) is so significant that the first three studies in Part Three are based on this material—and the same, central theme is repeated in each of them. This is not a printing error; it is fundamental to CM that collaboration with the Holy Spirit is understood.

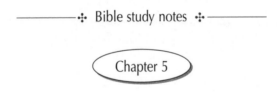

Bible study notes

Chapter 5

SOME LESSONS FROM ACTS

STUDY 1

Central theme

The main aim of this study is to consider that central to Christianity is collaboration with God. Every aspect of life is either a co-mission or a no-mission!

Bible passage

Read John 15:26—16:16 and then ask the following questions:

1. Jesus speaks of people recognizing their guilt, acknowledging their sin and accepting judgment. Can we think of three people in the Gospels who respond to Jesus in this way? Can we think of three people who don't?
2. Jesus says that in the future, the Holy Spirit will prompt people to respond in this way. In daily life, what does this mean?
3. Why does Jesus say that it is better for him to go and for the Spirit to come? What could be better than having Jesus right here, right now?

Bible passage

Read Acts 2:1–13.

1. Why does a crowd gather? What sense do they make of what they see?
2. What would probably have happened if neither Peter nor any of the other believers had said anything to the crowd?

Read Acts 2:14–37. Make a list of the key elements that Peter includes in his speech and then ask:

1. Do Peter's words cut *us* to the heart? If we went into town on Sunday and read this speech to a crowd, what effect do we think it would have?
2. Why does it cut these listeners to the heart? What light does John 16:8 cast on verse 37?

Read Acts 2:38–47.

1. How do people respond? What are they promised? What happens to them?
2. If we recognize this passage as the fulfilment of Jesus' promise in John 16, does this make sense? If the disciples are working in partnership with the Holy Spirit, can we think of Peter 'speaking to the ear' as the Holy Spirit 'speaks to the heart'? Can we think of examples of this kind of partnership that we have experienced? What does this tell us about collaborative ministry?

Time for prayer

Let's give thanks for our church. Let's pray for those in leadership and for all those whom the Holy Spirit will prompt into word and action.

To think about

God chooses to collaborate with the church: what if we fail to collaborate with him?

Closing passage

Read Matthew 28:18–20.

Bible study notes

Chapter 5

SOME LESSONS FROM ACTS

STUDY 2

Central theme

The main aim of this study is to consider that central to Christianity is collaboration with God. Every aspect of life is either a co-mission or a no-mission!

Bible passage

You will be studying Acts 8:26–40, but don't read it straight through. Instead, consider the story from two different perspectives—Philip's and the eunuch's. You could either split into two groups and, after an agreed time, tell each other the story from your character's point of view, or remain as one group, considering each story individually and then comparing them. Return to one group to consider the perspective of the Holy Spirit.

Philip's story

Try to imagine what this incident might have looked like from Philip's point of view:

Verse 26: Where is Philip? What is he doing? What level of detail does he receive in the angel's message?

Verse 27:	What does he do?
Verse 29:	What level of detail is he given now?
Verse 30:	What does he do? What initiative does he take?
Verse 35:	What is his own experience?
Verse 38:	What decision does he take?
Verses 39–40:	What does he know about the Ethiopian's future?

The eunuch's story

Try to imagine what this incident might have looked like from the Ethiopian's point of view:

Verses 27–28:	The man was a royal official in the palace of a queen; hence the operation! But he was also a 'proselyte' or convert, who had been to worship in Jerusalem. What has been going on during his stay in Jerusalem? (Check with Acts 6; 7 and 8:1–3.) What conclusions might he have come to?
Verse 31:	What is he doing? What is his reaction to the man who is walking beside his carriage?
Verses 34, 36:	What happens?
Verse 39:	What happens? What does he do?

Now let's speculate and consider this story from the point of view of the Holy Spirit. Try to imagine how the incident might be told from this third perspective.

The Lord's story

Using the information known from Philip's story... and the information known from the Ethiopian's story... imagine the Spirit narrating the story of how he brought these two men together and what happened. How would this third story be told?

Actually, there is always more than one story behind any incident. Consider:

- Our personal story of finding faith.
- The story of the person who brought us to faith.
- The Holy Spirit's story: how he brought us and the other person together, and how he spoke to and through us both.

Time for prayer

Let's pray for those who are not yet ready to hear. Let's pray for those who are ready but have no one to help them. Let's ask God to provide willing helpers.

To think about

Have we learnt the difference between God's prompting and our imagination?

Closing passage

Read Acts 1:8.

Bible study notes

Chapter 5

SOME LESSONS FROM ACTS

STUDY 3

Central theme

The main aim of this study is to consider that central to Christianity is collaboration with God. Every aspect of life is either a co-mission or a no-mission!

Bible passage

Read Acts 10:1–48.

1. Can we separate the verses so that they tell this story from three different points of view?
   - How would Cornelius tell the story?
   - How would Peter tell the story?
   - Is it possible to speculate about how the Holy Spirit would tell this story?

2. Is there collaboration between Peter and the Holy Spirit?

3. What is going on between Cornelius and the Holy Spirit?

4. In what ways is this passage similar to Acts 2 and Acts 8?

5. In what ways is it different?

Bible passage

Read Acts 11:1–18.

1. How do other Christians react to Peter's visit to Cornelius? Why?
2. How is the issue resolved?
3. What do we learn about 'life in the Spirit' from Acts 10 and 11?
4. Does this accord with our own experience?

Time for prayer

Let's pray for those who step out in faith and get it right. Let's also pray for those who step out in faith and get it wrong. Let's pray for those who have the task of discerning the difference.

To think about

What is the difference between inspiration and vision?

Closing passage

Read John 12:49.

Bible study notes

Chapter 6

A HOLY PRIESTHOOD

Central theme

The aim of this study is to consider our understanding of priesthood—to consider our theology and where in the Bible we locate it.

Bible passages

Consider this diagram of 'priesthood' (which could apply to any religion) where the priest occupies the role of an intermediary between the god and the people:

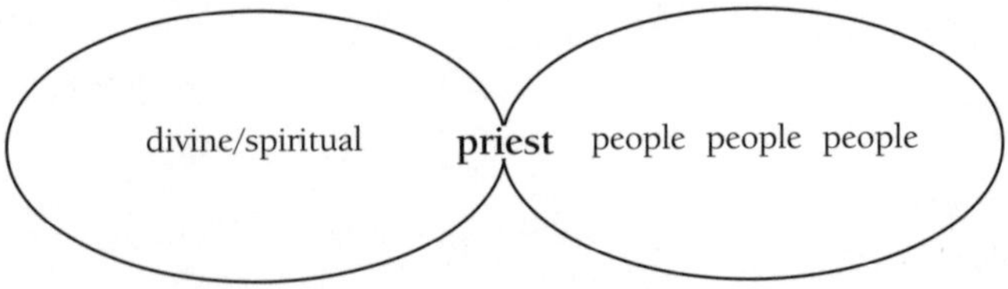

With this diagram in mind, ask: how do each of the following fulfil a priestly, intermediary role between God and the world?

- Human beings as described in Genesis 1:26–28.
- Abraham (Genesis 12:1–3).
- The Hebrew nation (Exodus 19:5–6).

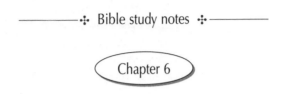

Bible passages

Read John 10:7–10 and 14:6.

- How does Jesus fulfil a priestly role?

The old covenant priesthood was located in the temple in Jerusalem. Read Matthew 24:1–2 and John 2:19.

- What does Jesus mean, and what are the implications for temple worship and the priesthood?

Read Mark 15:38.

- The curtain separated the Holy of Holies from the rest of the temple, and the world. What is the significance of the rip? In what ways does this impact on the concept of priesthood?

Bible passages

Read Hebrews 8:1–7; 9:11–28.

1. How did Paul understand priesthood, the temple and sacrifice?
2. In what ways does Jesus fulfil (rather than replace) the old covenant (Matthew 5:17–20)?

Read 1 Peter 2:5, 9.

1. How does Peter understand priesthood, the temple and the 'chosen nation'?
2. When the diagram above is considered, who in the New Testament occupies the place of 'priest'? In practice, what does this mean?
3. Referring to the diagram, ask: in what sense is new covenant priesthood the same as God's original pattern of creation (Genesis 1:26–28)?
4. In what ways is it different?

The contemporary church

Think about your own church.

1. In what sense (speaking practically) is Jesus Christ our high priest?
2. Do we call our leaders 'priests' or something else? Does it matter what we call them—is it their title which defines them or their role?
3. If we relate the 'priestly diagram' to our church, who occupies the 'priestly role'? Is it one person, several or everyone? Is our pattern of leadership (priesthood) old covenant or new covenant?

Time for prayer

Let's pray for our leaders—for the assistants, the main leader and the overseers.

To think about

Our understanding of leadership shapes our understanding of membership. How does our attitude to the one affect our approach to the other?

Closing passage

Read Revelation 1:5–6.

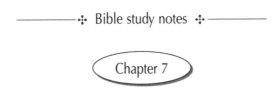

Bible study notes

Chapter 7

THE HOUSEHOLD OF FAITH

Central theme

The main aim of this study is to identify the head of the household—our authority. When it's Jesus, our attitude to leadership is different (as he said it would be).

Bible passages

Read Ephesians 3:14–15; 1 John 2:9–11; James 2:15–17; 1 Timothy 5:1–2.

1. Why do New Testament Christians think of each other in 'sibling' terms?
2. In New Testament terms, what was the difference between a household and a family?
3. What are the differences between our contemporary attitudes towards the 'Christian family' and New Testament attitudes towards the 'household of faith?'
4. Who is in charge of the both the church family and household? In practice, what does this mean?

Bible passages

Read Acts 2:43–47; 4:32–37.

1. Is the early church behaving as a family or a household? If there's a difference, what is it?
2. What is their experience of, and attitude towards, authority (Acts 5:1–11)?
3. When given the choice, whom do they obey (Acts 4:18–21, 31)? Why?
4. What does this tell us about their understanding of 'the head of the household'?

Bible passages

Read 1 Corinthians 3:1–3.

1. Is family life always easy? What happens when family members row?
2. Should we expect 'church family life' to be easy? What happens when Christians row?
3. In a 'natural family', what are the differences between children and adults? What about in the church (v. 2)? How can these differences be handled with Christian love?
4. In what ways are our attitudes to leadership mature or childish? In what ways are they shaped by Christian values or secular thinking (v. 3)?

Time for prayer

Let's pray for those who struggle at home. Let's pray for those who struggle at church.

To think about

In terms of church leadership, there is only one lesson in the New Testament imagery of the household of faith, and the Christian family: God is in charge.

Closing passage

Read John 13:34–35.

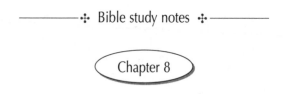

Bible study notes

Chapter 8

THE BRIDE OF CHRIST

Central theme

The main aim of this study is to differentiate the church as it is in the present from the future that we look forward to—and to consider the problems that arise when the future is confused with the present.

Bible passage

Read Isaiah 62:5 and then answer the following questions:

1. As a 21st-century bride approaches her wedding, what are her expectations?
2. As a 21st-century groom approaches his wedding, what are his expectations?
3. In first-century Israel, as a bride or groom approached their wedding, what would their expectations of marriage have been? (If you are not certain what first-century culture was like, thinking of rural Third World cultures today may help.)
4. If the biblical image of marriage between God and his people is viewed through first-century eyes, what is the image telling us about our relationship with God?.

Bible passages concerning the bride

Look up the following passages: Isaiah 49:18; Isaiah 61:10; Isaiah 62:5; Luke 5:33–35; John 3:27–30; Revelation 21:2–4; Revelation 22:17.

These are the significant passages that refer to the 'bride'. Let's ask two questions of them:

1. Do any of these passages speak of a present relationship? What aspects of a future relationship do they refer to?
2. Thinking about the picture of the future Jerusalem (meaning the capital, the central place of God's own people) and the bride being perfected to live there, what does this mean for the church in the present day?

Bible passages concerning the husband

There are a number of passages in the Bible that use this metaphor to describe God's relationship with his people. Here are some examples: Hosea 1:2; Jeremiah 3:6–13; Joel 1:8; Matthew 12:39; Mark 8:38.

1. Do any of these passages describe a future relationship? What aspects of the present relationship do they refer to?
2. In what terms is the people's behaviour described? What does this mean?

Bride and husband

Try to sum up this imagery as follows:

- Passages about the 'bride': what kind of relationship (and when) does this image describe?
- Passages about the 'husband': what kind of relationship (and when) does this image describe?

With this summary in mind, look at Ephesians 5:25–28.

1. In what ways does the imagery of marriage, bride and husband shape our understanding of church?
2. Does our understanding change if we interpret these images through the cultural filters of the first or 21st centuries?
3. What impact does this have on our understanding of church leadership and membership?

Time for prayer

Has our church been unfaithful? If yes, in what ways? In what ways is our church being prepared as the bride?

To think about

- Who are we trying to please in the things we do as a church?
- Picture a young bride with something on her face near her eye. The groom is reaching to pick it off and saying, 'Just stay still... I'll get it for you, but you must keep still!' Does this apply in any way to our church?

Closing passage

Read Isaiah 54:5. As the first-century bride hoped for a kind, loving husband (and imagine her delight when he was), so we hope that God will be kind and loving. How delightful to find that he is!

Bible study notes

Chapter 9

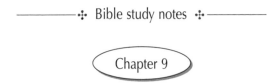

A SPIRITUAL TEMPLE

Central theme

This study considers the church in temple terms, as the place where God is worshipped, known and met, and where the Commandments are kept (lived) corporately.

Bible passage

Read 1 Peter 2:4–5.

1. Either consider the construction of a contemporary stone 'temple' or, preferably, visit one (perhaps the local church?). Ask these questions:
   - How many different shapes of stone can we identify?
   - What are the jobs of these different stones?
   - Are some stones more noticeable than others?
   - Are there hidden stones that we cannot see? What do they do?
   - Are all stones the same shape?

2. If Christians are living stones, built into a spiritual house (or temple), can we make a list of all the different types of stone in a building and relate each one to a different 'ministry'?

More Bible passages

Various passages refer to 'stones'.

1. In Exodus 31:18, the Ten Commandments are written on stone tablets.
    - In Ezekiel 36:26–27, what does God promise to do?
    - Are the Christians of 1 Peter 2:4–5 the living embodiment of Ezekiel's prophecy? If so, what does it mean to be a 'living stone'?

2. In 1 Kings 6, Solomon builds the temple. It is the place where God dwells among the people, where the stone tablets of the Commandments are kept, where all sacrifices are made and where sin is dealt with. There was only one temple.
    - In Ezekiel 37:25–28, God promises an abiding temple. Is this yet to come or a present reality?

3. In John 2:19, Jesus refers to himself as the temple. To understand this image, compare what the temple was with who Jesus was—Emmanuel, which translates as 'God with us'.
    - How does the idea of 'God with us' link to the temple?
    - In Matthew 24:1–2, Jesus predicts the destruction of Jerusalem's temple. In John 2:19–21, he predicts his own destruction and affirms that he will build 'the temple' again in three days. What is he talking about, and how will this affect temple worship?

4. In 1 Corinthians 3:16–17, Paul says that Christians are now the temple.
    - Both here and in 1 Peter 2:4–5, why is 'being church' a corporate activity?
    - What does it mean for the Christian church to be the new temple?

David Robertson, *Collaborative Ministry*, BRF, 2007

5. 1 Peter 2:6–8 refers to Jesus as the cornerstone—or a stumbling block.
   - What happens to the church if the keystone, Jesus, is missing? Is it possible to have a church without Jesus?

6. Ephesians 2:19–22 refers to building the church.
   - Who builds it? What does this mean?
   - What is the task of individual Christians (Jude 20–23) and how does this relate to Ephesians 2?

Living stones

1. If 'the temple' is no longer a man-made construction but a spiritual reality, in what senses does a gathering of living stones built upon the one cornerstone (Christ) fulfil a temple remit?
2. If the temple is 'where God is met', what does this mean for the church?
3. If the Commandments of God are kept in the 'new temple', what does this mean in practice?
4. If this is where sin is dealt with, what does this mean?
5. If a person becomes a living stone, where will they be built in?
6. What does this imagery mean in reality, and does the size of the church or the facilities on offer matter (Matthew 18:20)?

A spiritual temple

1. Who are the priests in this temple? What is their ministry?
2. Does this image give any guidance about how to organize different ministries?
3. If 'living stones' are diverse, are there any 'shapes' that cannot be built into the structure? If so, why not?
4. Will the available stones dictate the shape of the temple, or will the stones need shaping in order to fit the building plans?

Time for prayer

Let's pray for those who don't fit in. Let's pray for those who prefer to demolish. Let's pray for those who seek out the church, seeking God.

To think about

Gossip is like throwing stones from a distance, but these stones are deadly, not living.

Closing passage

Read 2 Thessalonians 2:3–4.

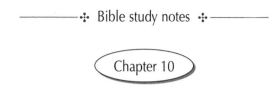

Bible study notes

Chapter 10

THE BODY OF CHRIST

Central theme

This study recognizes that Christ is risen and ascended, and considers the impact of the Holy Spirit in the church.

Group exercise

Describe the functions of the body of Christ. What does the body do? This can be answered in two ways:

- Talk about the body as it is described in 1 Corinthians 12:12–26.
- Talk about Jesus' body—which was born, drank milk, grew up, was crucified and so forth.

Both functions are valid because the incarnation is about God dwelling in flesh.

The incarnation

When we think of the incarnation, we rightly think of Jesus—God made human. We tend to forget, however, that God always makes himself known in a fleshly, incarnate way. Look at these passages.

1. Genesis 1:26–27: God makes human beings in his own image.
    - In what sense is this incarnational?

2. Romans 5:12–17: Paul speaks of the first Adam and the second Adam.
    - In what ways is the pattern of incarnation the same? In what ways is it different?

3. Genesis 12 onwards: God calls Abram and redemption begins. God chooses a couple, who become a family, who become a nation, to bring redemption.
    - In what ways does this follow an incarnational pattern?

4. Romans 4:13–16: Paul speaks of the offspring of Abraham.
    - What incarnational parallels does Paul draw between then and now?

5. Luke 1:26–38: The angel makes an announcement to Mary.
    - How is this incarnational intervention of God similar to the previous passages? How is it unique?

6. John 14:9–15: Jesus promises that his disciples will continue his ministry.
    - What does this tell us about Jesus' understanding of what will happen in the future?
    - How will God still interact incarnationally with his creation?

The body of Christ

Read Romans 12:4–5 and 1 Corinthians 12:12–26. Compare the two passages and list the points being made about the church.

- What does this tell us about the nature of the body?
- If God wants to reach Joe Bloggs, how will he do it?

The body of Christ has a pulse of its own, the Holy Spirit, and there are gifts for the task.

Bible passages

Read Romans 12:6–8 and 1 Corinthians 12:27–30. Compare the lists of gifts.

- If this is God's way of incarnation, should we expect all the gifts to be present in the church? Who can we identify as bearing these gifts in our church? Are there any gaps? Are there some gifts that seem not to be present? If so, why is this? If gifts are absent, what does it mean for the body?

Bible passage

Read Galatians 5:22–26.

- Compare the list of spiritual fruit with the list of spiritual gifts. What are the differences between the two?

Body ministry

In what ways does our understanding of the church as the body of Christ affect our approach to leadership and membership?

Time for prayer

Let's ask the Holy Spirit to grow spiritual fruit in our lives and increase the spiritual gifts given to our church.

To think about

Are the spiritual gifts we desire the same as the gifts God most wants to give?

Closing passage

Read James 2:14–17.

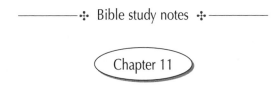

Bible study notes

Chapter 11

NEW COVENANT PEOPLE

Central theme

The main aim of this study is to consider the meaning of covenant and the response of new covenant people.

Old Testament passages

A covenant is a 'contract or mutual agreement'. In scripture, a covenant always has two sides.

Read Genesis 6:17–21 and 17:1–21. In these covenants:

- What does God promise to do for Noah and Abraham?
- What are they required to do for God?

There are many such passages. Covenant can be understood as an alliance, so what did it mean for Abraham to be a 'friend' of God (2 Chronicles 20:7)?

- If the old covenant is summed up in the phrase 'I will be your God, you will be my people', what happens when the people break the covenant?
- Does this explain God's frequent judgment on his 'unfaithful people'?

New Testament passages

1. During the Last Supper, where does Jesus 'locate' the new covenant (Mark 14:22–25)? What does this mean in practice?
2. In what sense does the new covenant supersede the old covenant (Hebrews 8:6–7)?
3. In what ways are the two covenants similar? In what ways are they different (Hebrews 12:24)?
4. Is the new covenant, like the old, a two-sided agreement? If so, what will God do for his people and what must his people do for him (Hebrews 13:20–21)?

An honest covenant

1. Does the contemporary church tend to highlight the benefits of the new covenant, while downplaying its reciprocal nature? Consider four passages:

- Matthew 11:28. Read verses 29–30 as well.
- Matthew 28:20b. Now read verses 18–20.
- Romans 8:28 (the whole verse, not just 'all things work together for good').
- 1 John 2:1. Now read verses 2–6.

2. Are any of these passages just about what God will do for us? What is required of us? Are these one-sided promises or facets of a two-sided agreement? What is the promise of God? What must we do to respond to him?

The example of prayer

Read Acts 4:1–31.

1. How did the early Christians understand their covenant relationship with God?

- What problems are the apostles facing?
- When released, what do they do?
- In their prayer, what do they ask for?

2. Is their expectation that God will change them so that they can respond to the situation like this?

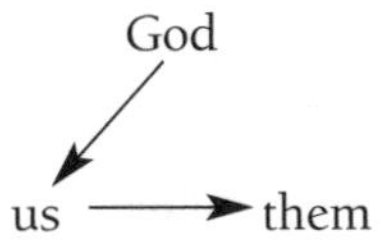

3. Does their attitude contrast with our own prayers? Do we ask God to change others without our physical involvement? Do we expect prayer to be answered like this?

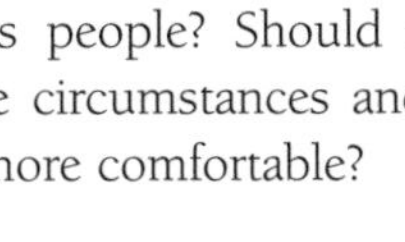

4. Which pattern of prayer reflects the 'covenant' relationship between God and his people? Should new covenant people expect God to change circumstances and people so that their lives are simpler and more comfortable?

5. Acts 4 says that God answered the prayer and demonstrated his presence, and the church continued to grow. Is it possible that some of our unanswered prayers and lack of growth are to do

with the way we pray? If our prayers are like the prayer in Acts 4, how does the church approach difficulties?

A new covenant church

1. If the new covenant is also summed up in the phrase 'I will be your God, and you will be my people', what does it mean to be 'bought for a price' (1 Corinthians 6:20; 7:23)?
2. What light does this covenant relationship shed on church leadership?
3. What does it teach us about church membership?
4. What does it tell us about the relationship between the leaders and members?

Time for prayer

Let's pray for one another—for a right attitude to God and for right attitudes with each other.

To think about

Does God exist to serve us or do we exist to serve him?

Closing passage

Read James 1:22–25.